A Song of Faith

plus The Gist of the Bible

James S. Wolfe

authorHOUSE®

AuthorHouse™
1663 Liberty Drive, Suite 200
Bloomington, IN 47403
www.authorhouse.com
Phone: 1-800-839-8640

First published by AuthorHouse 3/11/08

ISBN: 978-1-4343-6210-0 (sc)

Library of Congress Control Number 2008900066

Printed in the United States of America
Bloomington, Indiana

This book is printed on acid-free paper.

Preface

Episcopal Archbishop James Pike said he did not believe the creed when it was said but believed it when it was sung. Religious truth, which is always symbolic rather than literal, often travels best couched in art. The question is not whether religious expression is true but whether it rings true, whether it illuminates and reveals and inspires and breeds commitment. If some things I offer, including 35 of my poems and several poems from other sources, resonate with you, that is good.

There is also plenty of science here. The aim is not to espouse but to demonstrate that religion and science are compatible. Religion creates no science but leagues with art to celebrate what science describes.

Religions pervert what their founders stand for, fight wars and heresy, do more harm than good. But that is irrelevant. You will not find dogmatic and imperialistic religion here but free thinking and loving.

Although some major strands are identified on the following page, this tapestry is seamless, undivided by headings. The work took shape as I was inspired, and it languished for a few years as I wrestled with wicca, finally resolving to keep from it what I liked as I do with all religions. The song ends with my credo, into which I sew threads from seven religions.

The whole song has been recorded and is available on a CD. The section on the Four Elements is available alone as part of a directed meditation preceded by relaxation; the author can come read this for groups too.

The first appendix contains four of the hymns I have written (music not present but available). The second appendix is my favorite children's sermon, "Different is Good," which also celebrates diversity.
Finally, there is "The Gist of the Bible," which enables a person to glean the highlights of the Bible by reading two chapters a week for a year. A commentary is supplied for each pair. This section has a preface of its and a weekly schedule of passages (after page 68).

It may seem audacious of me to write up my thinking and poetry in a book. Why me? Well, why not? And why not you? As Marianne Williamson says in her poem (p. 37), "There's nothing enlightened about shrinking so that other people won't feel insecure around you." Do it!

Some Major Themes

I have heard with my own ears stories of faith. I have come across facts and theories. In my own way I try to make sense[1] of the world in which I live and of my place in it as a human in 2007 A.D. living in the United States, who is white, male, omnisexual, married, and a father, who holds a PhD in Religion and Society and a Master of Science in Computer Science, who worked as a computer programmer, a sociology professor, and a Presbyterian minister, who likes to play tennis, sing, write poems, and agitate for justice, who has lived on planet earth for 68 years and--should I live a century--will live here another 32 years before death.

I sing of faith. Faith is not believing the unbelievable; faith is not credulity. You cannot believe everything you hear. Disbelief is an ally of faith. Faith uses doubt to winnow chaff from wheat in the search for truth. Faith is not a source of new or arcane information. Instead faith yields a perspective on what we know. Faith is trust. The foundations of faith are laid in early infancy when a child does or does not receive the love and nourishment needed, comes to see the world as a basically good or bad place, develops an attitude of trust or mistrust. Faith expands and is tested by knowledge and experience. Faith is Abraham setting off for an unknown land of promise. Faith is Ann Frank believing in spite of everything that deep down humans are good. Faith is Jesus of Nazareth on a cross commending his spirit into his Father's hands. Faith is Isaac Newton and Albert Einstein doing science in order to think God's thoughts after him. Faith is confidence. Faith is getting up when morning has broken and greeting the new day as a time to be creative.

We live in time, and time lives in us. We live in natural time and historical time and personal time. Change in our universe is perennial, but social change seems especially accelerated in our era. Everywhere there is movement. Nothing stands still. Even in the mountains the electrons are dancing. One steps not twice in the same river. There are no things, only processes. There are no unions, only unitings and separations and reunitings.[2] Nothing endures forever.

---

[1] According to Paul Tillich, the problem of evil in the modern world focuses on meaninglessness in contrast to (now outdated) medieval preoccupation with guilt and ancient concern with finitude and death.

[2] There may be college reunitings, but there are definitely no college reunions. Those who gather are not the same people one once knew nor is the world they inhabit the same as it was.

Humans especially are continually redefining themselves. Trying for permanence instead is futile.[3] Craving to be complete instead of accepting the transitoriness of our living breeds unnecessary suffering, as Buddha noted.[4] Only embraced as wind and spirit are divinity and humanity immortal.

> Nothing remains but the wind in the willows,
> Billowing clouds sailing by in the sky,
> Mightily trying to blanket the universe,
> Bursting with energy never to die.
>
> Nothing endures of the world's grim scenario:
> Scary oppressors go down to defeat,
> Cheated of empires and fortunes magnificent,
> Driven to dust by the wind's ceaseless beat.
>
> Join in the process of living triumphantly.
> Gently cajole the recalcitrant power.
> Lower your sights from completing grand monuments;
> Ferment the grapes in the vat where you are.
>
> Spirit is life, is the only invincible;
> Sybil sings everything else to its death.
> Faith knows no permanent solid foundation stone,
> Only the wind dancing free in your breath.[5]

Our universe is comprised of bodies in motion within a vast sea of empty space. It has been around for a very long time and will continue for a very long time. There may have been a time when the universe was nothing but an infinitely dense black hole which expanded rapidly in a burst of light and motion. From this chaotic beginning, the stars and planets that spangle the heavens settled into regular courses--with occasional bursts of chaos such as meteors.

---

3 According to Jean Paul Sartre, humans have no substantial being but as centers of consciousness are holes in being; humans are "condemned to be free"--to project themselves anew into the future--while seeking a settled identity is a "useless passion."

4 According to Gautama Buddha, "life is suffering" (First Noble Truth) and "the source of suffering is craving" (Second Noble Truth); the solution lies in "non-striving" (Third Noble Truth), accepting our life as it is.

5 This is a poem of mine entitled "Wind." Note that both the Hebrew word *ruah* and the Greek word *pneuma* mean both "wind" and "spirit." Jesus says that the Spirit is like the wind, not visible in itself but visible in its effects.

According to the Greeks, after Night and Chaos, the first-born of the gods was Eros. They saw an erotic relationship among heavenly bodies in their mutual attraction and repulsion as the stars danced together. They believed that Love makes the world go 'round. The apparent fixity of stars in their constellations yields a wonderful feeling that we live in an intelligently patterned, or "logical," world.[6] So impressed were the Greeks with celestial harmony that they listed Uranus, patron of astronomy, among the Muses. Modern astronomers note that stars are in the process of burning themselves out. Our sun, for instance, as it produces the heat and light on which we depend, keeps converting mass into energy as it transforms hydrogen into helium through nuclear fusion. Some time the last star will expire.

When "the candles in the church are out" and "the lights have gone out in the sky", we can still "blow on the coal of the heart."[7] Love is first and last and in between. Love is divine. Love never dies. Love subjects itself to mortality and by enduring overcomes it.[8]

Out of the womb of Nothing something came,
Raging chaos stilled by streams of light;
Breath of heaven into dust took flight,
Gave to earth an order and a name.
Word made flesh, entombed in human frame,
Banished forever from heaven's perfect might,
God-forsaken, emptied, lost in night,
Suffering through our sorrow, pain, and shame.

Mourning, we greet his infernal triumph's comfort:
Gladly, we hail his eternal dying form.
Faithful to earth, embracing the Spirit's consort,
Wedded forever to flesh that is fresh and warm.
Requiem aeternam, deus est mort:
Long live he whose love survives the storm.[9]

---

[6] The Gospel of John begins by stating that "in the beginning was the Word;" this creative word comes forth from God and is God himself speaking, expressing himself as he calls the universe into being. The Hindus see playfulness in divine creativity. James Wendell Johnson sees a divine need for companionship. The night sky evokes wonder. Said Emmanuel Kant, "Two things fill me with wonder: the starry sky above and the moral law within."

[7] These phrases come from the end of Archibald MacLeish's play, JB.

[8] John of Patmos asserts that Christ is Alpha and Omega (Rev. 1:8). I John 4:8 states that "God is love." St. Paul in I Cor. 13 sees love outlasting everything else.

[9] This is a poem of mine entitled "Christus Victor." It draws some on Nietzsche.

I had a childhood friend who died of cancer shortly after being accepted into the New York Philharmonic Orchestra. I pondered the tragic loss involved in her death but also celebrated the quality of her short life and the eternal beauty she had created.

I Her viola lies in its case now,
   No fingers to caress its strings
   Into a soaring melody.

   Her body lies in its grave now,
   Her delicate fingers stilled,
   Bereft of song.

II The wicked worm doth bring to nought
   The budding genius as the common oaf.
   Fell, wanton death eats out the dream,
   Forecloses the ambition, denies
   The Gospel tinged with Zarathustra,
   Man longing to be superman.

   Yet in the end it is fair Jesu
   Who fills the joy of man's desiring.
   Yea, all our hopes and deeds receive
   In him their glory and their crown.

III She is here and then is gone
   Like music so soon lofted into air
   And lost to memory,
   Insubstantial, graceful, swift,
   Like footsteps running on the street
   Echoing, disappear in morning mist.

   Man, like music, lives in time,
   And time respects no man's fame.
   Great men's proud stone monuments
   Also wear away to sand.

   But "a thing of beauty is a joy forever"--
   So the saying goes--and so a chord,
   Once struck, is immortal, creating
   As it dies, a lasting note.
   "All things shall perish from under the sky.
   Music alone shall live, never to die."

IV   If in our brief time, some thing
Of beauty comes, some act of grace,
Count it all worth the candle.
Measure life by its quality,
Not its length, by its spirit,
Not its weight. For though we are
Mere wisps of Nothingness in the sea of being,
Frail creatures of dust and wind,
Tossed about amid the vagaries of earth,
Yet in that strange brief alchemy,
That lostness churning in chaotic whirls,
The God-breath comes to life in us,
And we though mortal live eternally in time,
And God's own life transfigures us sublime.[10]

The vastness of the universe is a source of wonder, but most of it is lifeless. Life, on however small a scale, is more wonderful; it is a miracle and a precious gift. Our planet earth originally was lifeless. It was a ball of superheated gases orbiting the star we call the sun, revolving on its own axis. This revolution makes sunlight available to some parts of the earth and absent from other parts during each spin. The spherical shape of earth makes the warmth of the sun more potent in the tropics and less so at the poles, and its tilt makes for some seasons being warmer and more conducive to life and growth than others.[11]

We experience the alternation of sunlight and darkness as day and night. Light is much praised as a source of actual illumination and as symbolic of divinity, knowledge, and goodness.[12] Darkness is excoriated as a source of stumbling and as symbolic of evil and benightedness. Yet light can blind and dark be the same as light.[13]

---

[10] This is a poem of mine entitled "Alison."

[11] The seasons have been named spring, summer, fall, and winter (in Western culture). The longest day occurs at the beginning of summer and the shortest at the beginning of winter (summer and winter solstices) while days and nights are equal at the start of spring and fall (vernal and autumnal equinoxes).

[12] I John asserts "God is light." The Gospel of John says that "the light that enlightens every person was coming into the world" as God's word took flesh in Jesus. The Book of Revelation envisions a world devoid of night. Reports of near-death experiences often contain an encounter with intense white light.

[13] Thus one cannot evade God by retreat to darkness (Psalm 139). The hymn "Immortal, Invisible" sings that "only the splendor of light hideth thee."

Night has its own allure as a time for play, imagination, risk, and mystery, as I express in the following poems:

Black Orpheus

I am a creature of the night
A light that flares and fades away,
A sprite that lurks till end of day
And then with dancing wings takes flight.
I am a creature warm and bright,
Delight to all whose lives are gray,
A wight whose plight is but to play
And make mock of sound and sight.

If all is plain, who cares to see?
If sun lays bare, where's modesty?
For knowledge scotches mystery.
But dark gives wings to fantasy.
And black gives birth to ecstasy,
'Tis night that makes a star of me.

Night Magic

Walking in the park at night
I fear, yet love, to hear the ducks
Splashing at the water's edge.

"Muggers stalk the park," they say,
"when day is spent." I cannot tread
Its walks without the dread of dark.

And yet the very darkness thrills
My routine soul to be alive
And walk alone where danger lurks.

The park is beautiful: the ducks,
The lighted temple dome, the pond,
The gilded monuments at rest.

And yet a single sound disturbs
My peaceful solitude--it jolts
My nerves and starts my heart to pound.

The eerie light induces fright
As shadows shroud the unseen beast
Who waits to pounce behind the hedge.

I run, I walk, I fear, I love,
I thrill, I dread, despair, delight--
How magical to walk at night!

Night

The sharp stillness of the night:
The black trees, the black earth, the black sky,
The rampant surge of the demiurge,
The gnarled cry of a hanging spy.

The bleary-eyed river, the mist,
The lost women, the vibrant wine,
The loud, ecstatic city,
The lonely pine.

The phantom car, the phantom speed,
The blaring drum-beat, the strangling weed,
Demonic beauty, ghastly light--
The fascination of the night.

Actually, we are blessed to have both night and day, darkness and light. They balance each other, as in the Chinese symbol yin/yang or Jung's theory of animus and anima. The darker sides of ourselves must come to light and be accepted if we are to lead integrated lives. Darkness is not destroyed by light but embraced and encompassed; light shines in the darkness, and the darkness has not overcome it.[14] Though it does not always correspond to day and night in a modern society with nocturnal illumination and night jobs, there is a time for work and a time for rest,[15] and a need to balance activity and contemplation.[16] There is also a need to express both enlightened rationality and dark passions, to honor both Apollo and Dionysius.

> Bereft of sense, outrageously besot,
> I join the company of knaves and fools
> From whom the lust of passion foully drools
> Like putrid juice from apples that have rot.
> I see a thousand silver lakes that dot
> The verdant landscape, calm reflecting pools,
> Set in the hills like irridescent jewels,
> Of freshing spring and quiet streams begot.
>
> I've coursed, enraptured, Dionysius' dance
> And heard the blessed strains of Apollo's lyre
> I've sung a tragic ode by plan and chance
> And spoken sparkling words by a roaring fire.
> Zagreus and Phoebus embraced in ecstatic trance
> While I danced to rhythmic chants of a heavenly choir.[17]

---

14 So concludes the prologue to the Gospel of John. Paul admonishes Christians not to overcome evil with evil but to overcome evil with good.

15 A Sabbath prayer extols: "Praised be Thou, O Lord our God, ruler of the world, by whose law the shadows of evening fall and the gates of morn are opened. In wisdom Thou hast established the changes of times and seasons and ordered the stars in their heavenly courses. Creator of heaven and earth, O living God, rule thou over us forever. Praised be Thou, O Lord, for the day and its work and for the night and its rest."

16 Medieval Catholicism reserved the contemplative life for monks and nuns though the Benedictines advised balance in their slogan, *ora et labora* (prayer and work). The Hindus reserve contemplation for old age when men of the world can become *sunnyasin* (holy men) detached from the world; wives may do likewise but no longer attached to their husbands. Martin Buber contends that the contemplative attitude should belong to all of us not as a retreat from the world but in the midst of lived life. Americans and their religion is more activist than contemplative. Daniel Berrigan gives them some sage advice: "the buddha says, 'Don't just do something; stand there."

17 My poem "Symposium" depicts a retreat both academic and convivial.

Night and day are not distinct but edge into each other without clear boundaries. Life is enriched when the lines are fuzzed.

There is no side, only side-by-side:
I'll walk side by side with anyone.
There is no fence, only self-defence:
I defend the right to be who I am becoming.
There is no wall, only walleye,
The fish my wife hasn't figured how to fix.

Some things are as "different as night and day,"
Yet night and day are not so different.
They flow into each other with plenty of buffer
As in the dawning of the sun I so seldom see
And in the twilight and sunset I cherish.
Clouds often obscure the sun as they dance before it,
And night can be spruced by a thousand points of light.

When God began to add his creative touch to the world,
She separated the seas from the dry land
But also mixed water and dirt
In the most fruitful parts of earth
And commingled them in the swamp.
I am not a clear stream cascading over rocks;
I own the swamp I am.

Why do we have to draw lines and distinctions and boundaries?
Are we afraid that something will get loose, spill over?
Are we too insecure to be permeable,
To take the hands of aliens in our own?
From fear we take sides, build fences, erect walls.
But perfect love casts out fear.
Let us live in love.

I dare to go where no man goes before.
I color outside the lines using all the colors of the rainbow.
I build bridges instead of fences.
I rook a rock here and there
And watch the walls come tumbling down.
I embrace the best of both worlds, of all worlds.
My cup runneth over.[18]

---

[18] I wrote this poem "Boundless" after starting to read <u>Bi Any Other Name</u>.

Over time the gases comprising our nascent earth cooled, an enveloping atmosphere took shape, the rains came and the floods; rivers, lakes, oceans, and dry land emerged as winds and rains abate. The general development of Earth runs from chaos to complexity, from blurred uniformity to the richness of variety; chaos is contained by order, yet chaos continues to erupt, as in extreme weather such as hurricanes, tornados, floods, and earthquakes.[19] There is a titanic beauty in these eruptions as well as great havoc. We might wish that chaos disappear, but a little bit of chaos is a key to creativity. Creation involves the shaping of that which is not into actuality,[20] turning raw material in all its potential power into a finite, finished product. A world in perfect order is perfectly boring, as Shaw says.[21] In the best of all possible worlds there is a balance between chaos and order, some golden mean between tumult and rigidity. Great art draws on both inspiration and discipline, spontaneity and structure, novelty and pattern. Great politics shakes up the political order with periodic revolutions (every twenty years in Jefferson's advice). Great lives strike a good balance between the energy of id and the restraint of superego, between passion and civility, between heart and head, the claims of Dionysius and Apollo. Dr. Jekyll and Mr. Hyde live in each of us in more or less benign conflict. I see this duality in myself:

> Head over heels in love am I.
> Heart over head to Darrell I fly.
> Soft in the head I throw cares to the wind.
> Warm in my heart I show care for my friend.
>
> Innocent, jaded, caring, carefree,
> Respectable burgher, child of the sea.
> Marked by contraries yet strangely whole,
> I love that man both body and soul...[22]

---

[19] It is ironic that insurance contracts refer to extreme weather exempted from coverage as "acts of God." John Wesley said, "There is no divine visitation which is likely to have so general an influence on sinners as an earthquake (Newsweek, 7/26/93, p. 46)." However, the biblical God is portrayed as one who brings order out of chaos (as in Genesis 1:1-3 "In the beginning when God began to create the heavens and the earth--when the earth was without form and void and darkness lay upon the face of the deep and a mighty wind raged over the face of the waters--God said, 'Let there be light,' and there was light.")

[20] Tillich tags chaotic non-being which is potential being as the Greek *me on*, Systematic Theology, vol. I, p 172. Whitehead infers a principle of concretion which enables ideas in the primordial mind of God to take definite shape.

[21] The general in "Man and Superman" prefers hell to the boredom of heaven.

[22] These lines come from my poem "To Darrell"

Life began imperceptibly in the sea, probably in a fragmentary way, in the form of simple microorganisms perhaps akin to bacteria and to viruses, which are lively in some settings and appear lifeless in others. Plants and animals emerged, eating and being eaten, reproducing and composting, some sedimenting into coal and oil.[23] The whole creation teems with diversity. Yet all of us are made of the same basic elements, which the Greeks identified as **fire, air, earth, and water.** The adventure of philosophy began when Thales claimed that the source of all things is water. We humans are mostly made of water, water as salty as the sea, and we need to drink lots of water to stay healthy. We emerge at birth from a watery womb, and the waters of baptism symbolize being born anew. Water derives its power from its weakness. When water is invaded it remains flexible, stepping aside to let the invader in and absorbing him, yet nothing is stronger than water, which creeps into the rocks and, freezing, breaks them apart. Lao Tsu reflected on this in the sixth century B.C.

> Under heaven nothing is more soft and yielding than water.
> Yet for attacking the solid and strong, nothing is better;
> It has no equal.
> The weak can overcome the strong.
> The supple can overcome the stiff...
> The softest thing in the universe
> Overcomes the hardest thing in the universe.
> That without substance can enter where there is no room...
> The highest good is like water.
> Water gives life to the ten thousand things and does not strive.
> It flows in places men reject and so is like the Tao...
> Tao in the world is like a river flowing home to the sea...
> Tao is the source of the ten thousand things. [24]

---

23 Says Ernest Becker (Denial of Death, p. 282): "The routine activity is for organisms to be tearing others apart with teeth of all types--biting, grinding flesh, plant stalks, bones between molars, pushing the pulp greedily down the gullet with delight, incorporating its essense into one's own organization, and then excreting with foul stench and gasses the residue. Creation is a nightmare spectacular taking place on a planet that has been soaked for hundreds of of millions of years in the blood of its own creatures. The soberest conclusion that we could make about what has actually been taking place on the planet for about three billion years is that it is being turned into a vast pit of fertilizer. But the sun distracts out attention, always baking the blood dry, making things grow over it, and with its warmth giving the hope that comes with the organism's comfort and expansiveness."

24 Excerpts from the Tao Te Ching, Numbers 78, 43, 8, 32, 62.

Water evaporates without a trace; it leaves no footprints. The person attuned to water meanders quietly, following the flow. One should ride along the waters of life like an empty boat; if someone runs into such a boat, there is no one to curse. No one can burst your bubble unless you are inflated. The quest to be outstanding is futile, and it isolates you from others. Rather seek to be at one with the universe, not dominating it as a separate self but in tune with it as part of it. As Jesus did not lord it over others but emptied himself, taking the form of a servant, taking the towel as he washed feet, poured himself out to save the world, and advocated that his followers do likewise, gaining life by spending it,[25] so also Lao Tsu disparages holding and clinging and trying to save one's life in favor of self-emptying:

> The universe is sacred.
> You cannot improve it.
> If you try to change it, you will ruin it.
> If you try to hold it, you will lose it...
> He who is attached to things will suffer much.
> He who saves will suffer heavy loss...
> Empty yourself of everything.
> Let the mind rest at peace.[26]

I had an experience of oneness with the ocean, an oceanic feeling of losing my separate self and being wonderfully engulfed:

> the ocean has a grandeur
> and the lonely gull a grace
> no cumbrous brush can trace
> nor windy words conjure
> silent at rest i injure
> no one in this sacred place
> lost in boundless space
> i nowhere venture
>
> crash wave
> break free
> make grave
> for me
> save
> sea [27]

---

[25] Phil. 2:7, John 13:5, Matt. 26:28, Matt. 16:25. The minister's stole represents Jesus' towel. Jesus said his disciples should wash each other's feet as he did.
[26] Excerpts from the Tao Te Ching, Numbers 29, 44, 16.
[27] This poem is named for its place of composition in California: "Aptos Beach."

Like water, the person of Tao nourishes all humbly and thus greatly:

> The great Tao flows everywhere, both to the left and to the right.
> The ten thousand things depend upon it; it holds nothing back.
> It fulfills its purpose silently and makes no claim.
> It nourishes the ten thousand things,
> And yet is not their lord.
> It has no aim; it is very small.
> The ten thousand things return to it,
> Yet it is not their lord.
> It is very great.
> It does not show greatness,
> And therefore is truly great.

> The Tao of heaven is like the bending of a bow.
> The high is lowered, and the low is raised.
> If the string is too long, it is shortened;
> If there is not enough, it is made longer.
> The Tao of heaven is to take from those who have too much
>   and to give to those who do not have enough.
> Man's way is different.
> He takes from those who do not have enough
>   to give to those who already have too much.
> What man has more than enough and gives it to the world?
> Only the man of Tao.
> Therefore the sage works without recognition.
> He achieves what has to be done without dwelling on it.
> He does not try to show his knowledge.

> Yield and overcome;
> Bend and be straight;
> Empty and be full;
> Wear out and be new;
> Have little and gain;
> Have much and be confused.
> Therefore wise men embrace the one
> And set an example to all.
> Not putting on a display, they shine forth.
> Not justifying themselves, they are distinguished.
> Not boasting, they receive recognition. [28]

---

28 Tao te Ching, Numbers 34, 77, 22. Creating without claiming / Doing without taking credit / Guiding without interfering / This is primal Virtue (51).

Likewise, Jesus said that he who would be greatest must be
servant of all. He said the last would be first and the first last.
He praised the widow's pennies above rich men's millions,
for they gave what they could spare while she gave all she had.
He disparaged greed saying that life is more than the abundance of
things possessed. He was hailed as an instrument of divine justice:

My soul magnifies the Lord,
and my spirit rejoices in God my Saviour.
He has shown strength with his arm,
he has scattered the proud in the imagination of their hearts,
he has put down the mighty from their thrones,
and exalted those of low degree;
he has filled the hungry with good things
and the rich he has sent empty away.[29]

Jesus declared his divine mission as raising those who are down:

The Spirit of the Lord is upon me,
because he has anointed me to preach good news to the poor.
He has sent me to proclaim release to the captives
and recovering of sight to the blind,
to set at liberty those who are oppressed,
and to proclaim the year of God's favor.[30]

Jesus befriended tax collectors and prostitutes, lepers and
demoniacs. He exhibited a love which is patient and kind,
encouraging and enduring, not insisting on his own way nor being
jealous or boastful, arrogant or rude. Jesus did not monopolize his
divine powers but freely shared them, expecting others to achieve
more than himself. He kept telling pointed stories and healing the
sick and gathering followers and exposing hypocrisy and giving hope,
even though it got him into trouble. Being arrested and executed
without resistance, he appeared weak and foolish. But the divine
weakness and foolishness proved stronger and wiser than the men
opposing it. Jesus is exalted because he did not exalt himself but
emptied himself utterly, not blocking but being transparent to divine
light shining through him.[31]

---

[29] Luke 1: 46-53. See also Mark 9:33-37 and Mark 10: 35-45; Matt. 19: 23-30 and
Luke 13:22-30; Mark 12: 41-44; Luke 12: 13-21.

[30] Luke 4:18-19 based on Isaiah 61: 1-2.

[31] See Matt. 11: 16-19; Matt. 11: 2-5; Matt. 9: 32-34; I Cor. 13: 4-7; I Cor 1: 18-31;
Phil. 2: 1-11. For Jesus as transparent, see Tillich, Syst. Theology, vol. I, p. 148.

As noted, we are mainly made of water. We are soft inside and moist. We should treasure our vulnerability and flexibility as we float easily upon the river of life. Rivers of blood flow through us marking our kinship with trees and streams:

> I know the sap that courses through the trees
> as I know the blood that flows in my veins.
> The shining water that moves in the streams and rivers is not
> simply water, but the blood of your grandfather's grandfather.
> The rivers are our brothers. They quench our thirst.
> They carry our canoes and feed our children.
> You must give to the rivers the kindness
> you would give to any brother.

Besides water, we are also made of earth. We are groundlings (*adam*) who come from the ground (*adamah*) and return to it. We should treasure ourselves as treasure-filled earthen vessels who replenish rather than ravage the earth from which we spring:

> Teach your children what we have taught our children,
> that the earth is our mother.
> Whatever befalls the earth befalls the sons of the earth.
> If men spit upon the ground,
> they spit upon themselves.
> The earth does not belong to man;
> man belongs to the earth.

> Let earth not know I have been here,
> Erect no tomb or monument
> That scars the hills with drear cement
> And turns the errant rain to tear.
> Preserve no marking by my bier,
> But let my buried excrement
> Become the treasured sacrament
> That feeds the earth what I held dear.

> Ashes to ashes and dust to dust,
> I came when I might and left when I must.
> Walked I softly and made no dent,
> In joy and peace my years were spent.
> I lived in love and cast out fear;
> I came, I saw--and then I went.[32]

---

32 This poem of mine is entitled "No Trace." The last line is in clear contrast to Julius Caesar's comment about Gaul: "I came. I saw. I conquered." See Gen. 2:7

The wet earth we are is vivified by air. It is not until the artful potter blows into the lump of clay she has shaped the breath of life that man becomes--like the other animals before him--a living being. In the divine creativity the winds of chaos are tamed into the breath of creatures. In and out we breathe continuously from birth to death.

> The air is precious.
> It shares its spirit with all the life it supports.
> The wind that gave me my first breath
> also receives my last sigh.[33]

The Hindus experience breathing as spiritual. *Atman* is *brahman*: my breath is the divine breath. Jesus breathed his spirit on his disciples, and baptism symbolizes being reborn of water and spirit. Those who walk in the spirit let the divine spirit blow through them like wind unseen in its origin and destination but known in its effects since spirit is known by its fruits; the answer is blowing in the wind. One must test the spirits, whether they are divine.[34] An ill wind blows no good. A harsh wind can blow us off course, but a gentle breeze can be an inspiration. Like the "rustling of leaves in the forest" in Schubert's "Omnipotence," I experienced the beauty of leaves in the breeze as divine in origin:

> Two birches by the ocean stand,
> Tall and white and delicate.
> Their leaves like drops of water wait
> To sprinkle on the sand.
> Their branches by the breeze are fanned;
> As moonbeams part each tiny gate
> 'Twixt twig and leaf and scintillate,
> Leaf shadows dance on sea and land.

---

[33] Attributed to Chief Seattle in Susan Jeffers' Brother Eagle, Sister Sky as are two previous passages about the rivers as brothers and earth as our mother. For God as potter, see Isaiah 64:8 and the hymn "Have thine own way, Lord." Earlier translations said "man became a living soul," seeming perhaps to distinguish man from animals, but the same Hebrew phrase *nephesh hayah* in Gen. 2:7 is also applied to animals in Gen. 2: 19 ("living creature" in RSV). Since the Hebrew *ruah* can mean either "wind" or "spirit," *ruah elohim* in Gen. 1:1 could be "Spirit of God" but is better rendered as "mighty wind."

[34] See John 20:22; John 3: 5, 8; I John 4:1. In Greek, as in Hebrew, the same word (pneuma) means both "wind" and "spirit" making John's analogy easy. "Blowing in the Wind" was a popular folk song in the Sixties. Suicide pilots in World War II were called kami-kaze ("divine wind") so watch what wind you fly! Paul hopes we will stop being blown by every wind of doctrine (Eph. 4:14).

Two birches by the ocean stand,
Tall, serene, and free.
In silence they speak to the starry band;
In silence they speak to me.
And in their beauty I see God's hand,
The hand that made the sea.[35]

Sea and land and air are there around us and within us. What is missing--or rather unnoted--is fire. Without fire all would be still and therefore lifeless. It is fire that turns air into wind and breath. The burning sun invites molecules of air to dance producing wind and stirs molecules of water to rise to heaven to fall again as rain. The sun is also catalyst to photosynthesis by which green plants make sugars. All our movement is fueled by burning the sugars we eat and store using oxygen from the air we breathe in and producing byproducts of carbon dioxide breathed out and water eliminated in urine and sweat.[36] Our heaving chests that force air in and out of our lungs and our beating hearts that force the blood to course through our brains, organs, and limbs enabling thinking, digestion, and locomotion bear witness to thousands of fires burning within us, even when we sleep. We heat up more when we engage in thought or work, make love, or run or dance:

A blazing flash of lightning, swift I flew,
My pirouettes untamed by fear or norm.
My nimble limbs were dancing up a storm.
My footsteps leaves swept round as whirlwinds blew.
Intoxicated by the witches' brew,
A spell enveloped my whole dancing form,
And, like a whirling dervish stoned, a warm
Perspiring juice bespangled me like dew.

When on a single thing we concentrate--
A task at work, a winning play, a dance--
Our energies are bent to pull the freight,
Our bodies supple, minds in tune. Perchance,
Forgetting self, absorbed, we will create
A masterpiece and all our lives enhance. [37]

---

35 I wrote this poem "Twin Birches" in high school after a lakeside reverie.
36 Sugars are compounds of carbon, hydrogen, and oxygen (CHO). Burning is adding more oxygen (oxygenization). The byproducts are CO_2 and H_2O.
37 This poem of mine is entitled "Dancer." I love to throw myself into dance.

It is said that the god Prometheus stole fire from heaven and gave it to men enabling the smelting of metals and the development of the technical arts. Our technological progress has been a blessing to humankind though it can also be a bane to humans and our planet. We are most alive when the fire of passion burns within us, most spirited when we would trade all for a pearl of great price, most fully human when engaged in a quest to discover or create or to overcome:

> 'Midst the mists the mountains rise,
> Proud, unconquered Lords of space.
> Edged with ice, each rugged face
> Sparks a challenge to our eyes.
> How the mountains tantalize
> Us 'round crevices to trace
> Paths to that mysterious place
> Seen triumphant in the skies!
>
> The mountains call; we cannot stop.
> Unconquered they shan't always be!
> Though we from heights to death may drop
> Or should return in misery,
> The joy of standing on the top
> Makes us chance all for victory. [38]

When we are energized by a supreme purpose, our lesser aims are burnt away as in a refiner's fire. We are baptized by a holy spirit and with fire. Our hearts burn within us or are strangely warmed when holy love abounds. [39] Love and life flare up and subside:

> Our love is such a fragile thing,
> A candle flame caressed by air,
> Which blows it bright and blows it fair
> Or blows it out as hope takes wing. [40]

When the fire is blown out in death, we achieve release (*nirvana*). You are dead as soon as the fire goes out--even before you expire. Soon after breathing stops. Body returns to earth as food for worms; blood flows out into the river of life. Behold all flesh is like grass. The grass withers; the flower fades. Only the divine speech goes on.

---

[38] I wrote "Because It's There" after climbing the Grand Teton at age 14.
[39] See Matt. 3:11; Luke 24:32. John Wesley's heart was "strangely warmed."
[40] This poem "A Flame" records the shifting love with a boyfriend.

Fire, air, earth, and water are involved in the life of all creatures, whose great variety bespeaks the infinite creativity of their source. Creatures vary by habitat. Some plants and animals live in the depth of the sea where no light comes and entrapped air is minimal while others thrive in shallower waters. Some burrow within the earth while others creep or walk upon its surface. Some fly or leap through the air alighting on land, water, trees, or lily pads. We celebrate the distinctive character of creatures and their habitats:

> On mighty wings uplifted soars the eagle proud
> With swift exulting flight to greet the sun.
> At morn the merry lark his cheerful welcome sings,
> And cooing calls the tender dove his mate.
> From every bush and grove
> Pours forth the nightingale's sweet carol:
> No grief has ruffled yet her breast,
> Nor yet to sorrow has been tuned her charming rondelay.
>
> In fairest raiment now with virgin green adorned,
> The rolling hills appear.
> From deep and secret springs in fleeting crystal flow
> The gurgling brook doth pour.
>
> In lofty circles play on wheeling tides of air the cheerful birds:
> Their glittering plumes are dyed as rainbows by the sun.
> See flashing through the deep in thronging swarms
> The fish who leap and twist in ceaseless motion round.
> From deepest ocean home the immense Leviathan
> Upheaves to sport upon the foaming wave.
>
> Triumphant roaring stands the lion.
> With a lightning leap the tiger appears.
> Bounding, the nimble stag bears up his branching head.
> With snorting and stamping, flying mane,
> Uprears in might the noble steed.
> In pleasant pastures quietly the cattle graze on meadows green
> And o'er the ground as if planted there
> Abide the fleecy, gentle sheep.
> Like clouds of dust, assembled swarms of insects buzz.
> In long dimension creeps, with sinuous trace, the worm.[41]

---

[41] Excerpts from Haydn's "Creation." See the litany in Gen. 1:20-25. Rather than being a scientific account of the origins of the world, it is a responsive reading read at New Year's to celebrate receiving the world anew from God.

Creatures evolve from other creatures. Something like the humble amoeba is great grandfather of us all. The amoeba eats by incorporating nutients into itself, and when it grows large enough, it reproduces by subdividing. Both subparts are genetically identical usually. Other species involve two parents in reproduction. Then the genetic composition of the offspring is a unique combination of inherited genes (usually). But every once in a while there will be a significant mutation in the genes of the offspring, and a mutant will emerge. Most mutants are deformed, and many die young. But occasionally a mutant individual will be better adapted to his environment than his predecessors and will prevail alongside or over them as he gives birth to a new strain or perhaps--over a series of mutations--to a new species. Thus by eating and reproduction, individual creatures and existing species survive, and from mutation new species arise. The survival of a species depends on its fitness. In the struggle for survival, those better adapted to environment fare better. Their fate depends on factors such as food supply, climate, strength, defenses, rate of reproduction, and intelligence.

Species come and go. Some have been perennial: one-celled plants and animals, viruses and bacteria, insects. One-celled critters are so simple and basic that they are largely impervious to changing conditions. Bacteria, viruses, and parasites enter into the struggle for survival using us and other animals as hosts. They aid digestion and decomposition but also bring disease and death, especially in poor countries. In more developed nations, better sanitation has curbed the proliferation of harmful bacteria, better nutrition has fortified bodies against them, and antibiotic medicines have neutralized them though overuse of antibiotics has wiped out certain strains and encouraged unaffected mutant strains to take their place. Insects spread germs, eat crops, and are food for birds. Some were in danger of being decimated by DDT, threatening the birds that depended upon them and auguring a silent spring: we use less toxic pesticides now though we continue to endanger farm workers and food consumers to a degree. Insects also outwit pesticides by developing mutant strains, so the endless battle against bugs needs to be evaluated for costs and benefits compared to more organic approaches to farming. Some insects have very short lifespans. Mayflies, for instance, hatch, mate, lay eggs, and die in the space of a day or two. Insects are vulnerable and expendable but prolific; they will probably outlast humans in the evolutionary scheme. In the meantime, we coexist with the simplest creatures in an uneasy truce deriving some benefits and trying to limit damage.

Some species flourish and die out. Massive mastodons once roamed the earth but are no more. Dinosaurs dominated our planet but could not survive a climate change, perhaps brought on by a meteor/comet colliding with Earth setting off volcanic activity. The dodo bird headed for extinction when it grew too fat to fly and thus became easy prey. In the short run, natural habitats tend to reach an ecological balance. Species do not die out, but as one sort of plant or animal proliferates or diminishes those who feast upon them likewise wax or wane. However, human civilization encroaches on wilderness and disrupts ecological balance. Destroying rain forests extinguishes rare species reducing diversity in creation and reducing our pharmacological resources. We humans are both products and caretakers of the evolutionary process. With Teihard de Chardin we embrace evolution as God's way of creating and see ourselves, as "man come of age," called by God to "grasp the tiller of the world." As stewards of earth and its creatures, we have a divine mandate to replenish the earth, even as we subdue it, [42] seeking to preserve the species we endanger and to provide a habitable environment for ourselves and our fellow creatures.

Man is the apex of the evolutionary process, crown of creation. We stand upon shoulders of predecessors, animal and human. From simpler creatures more complex creatures evolve. For instance, warm-blooded birds serenade us even though the cold-blooded flying dinosaurs from which they emerged have ceased to be. It is surmised that we ourselves evolved from a lost ancestor common to us and some apes (though such an ancestor has not yet been dug up). Before our hominid forebears came down from the trees and became carnivorous, they feasted on fruits, as monkeys do, and some would suggest that we would be better off fruitarian and vegetarian since it is inefficient to send nutrition from grains through animals to us. We are not so different from other animals. Like many living beings, we are creatures of dust and breath: inspiring, aspiring earthlings.[43] Like all actual entities, we have both physical and mental poles (Whitehead). Like more advanced animals, we engage in mental processes: perception, moods, deceit, pondering, choice. We humans are gifted with especially developed intelligence, aiding our survival.

---

[42] Genesis 1:28.

[43] See Genesis 2:7. Though translators have used special phrases such as "living soul (KJV)" or "living being (RSV)," in the Hebrew text *nephesh hayah* is used for both humans and other animals, who were seen as man's first companions; this phrase is translated as "living creatures (RSV)" in Gen 2:19.

Although humans are distinguished from other animals by superior intelligence and cultural accomplishments, we share their infirmities. Human sin abets disease and death, but we did not bring them into the world. Disease and death were here before humans; they are part of our evolutionary heritage. Like the other animals from which we have evolved, we are liable to malformation, injury, disease, and death. While death might be absent in a more perfect world, it is as natural as life in the world in which we live. Through death and reproduction, nature replenishes herself by laying aside old deteriorated bodies and bringing in new creatures. There are natural cycles of running, fortune, weather, seasons, light, and life:

> Old sweat to new sweat
> On the filthy old shirt.
> A bit wet, now quite wet
> And splattered with dirt.
>
> Good health to poor health,
> Thence to disease.
> Small wealth to less wealth
> And drear miseries.
>
> White clouds to black clouds,
> Black clouds to rain.
> Sad crowds and white shrouds,
> Death comes again.
>
> Gray night to black night,
> Ruin and decay.
> A faint light to dawn's light
> To the brightness of day.
>
> Old life to new life,
> A baby cries.
> Fall's strife to spring's fife:
> Life never dies. [44]

Death itself is not our enemy, and we waste much effort and money in futile attempts to postpone it. Prolonging life in a vegetative state by artificial means at great expense makes no sense. How much better to say with Saint Francis, "Welcome, Brother Death!"

---

[44] I wrote this poem "Changes" in high school after a rainy crosscountry race.

Most babies are born well-formed and healthy; some are not. We should let babies die who are so poorly formed or so diseased that they have no chance of surviving infancy. Better yet we should see that the birth of premature, low birth-weight, disease-prone babies is minimized by providing adequate pre-natal nutrition and care for pregnant women, and we should allow the abortion of grossly deformed fetuses. Abortion is also surely allowable in the cases of violation of choice (rape), probable concentration of genetic flaws (incest), and danger to the life and health of the mother. Abortion involves the taking of a life, a potentially human life, and it should not be chosen lightly or without due consideration of alternatives such as giving the baby for adoption. Yet it is better to abort the fetus--the sooner, the better--than to neglect the child it would become. Better yet it is to avoid conception through timing of intercourse or through contraception when a child is not wanted. Once a child is born, we are obliged--as parents and as a society-- to care for it regardless of our wishes or its defects. As Jesus said in regard to a man born blind, it is not appropriate to blame anyone or to stigmatize the disabled, who should be afforded as full a life as possible in face of the conditions which challenge them. [45]

As soft-shelled, air-breathing creatures, we are liable to injury. We should minimize injury by reducing pollution, dangerous working conditions, unsafe homes, domestic disputes, contact sports, drunk driving, excessive speeding, armed robberies, gang wars, hate crimes, militia bombings, international terrorism, and military warfare.

Disease in animals and humans stems from several sources, such as genes, germs, and degeneration. Little can be done to stop inherited disease, but good nutrition and sanitation can reduce the prevalence and potency of germs as well as slow degeneration. There is much we can do for our health by cutting out or down on alcohol and other drugs, smoking, obesity, stress, and unsafe sex. Our bodies are temples of the divine spirit. [46] We are responsible for taking care of our own health and fostering the health of others, including seeking medical treatment when appropriate and visiting those who are sick. Reduced health from aging eventually takes its toll, but it need not prevent the elderly from leading full, productive lives for many years. Organs deteriorate over time, and tumors crop up. When we are too far gone, we should be allowed to die in peace.

---

[45] See John 9:1
[46] See I Corinthians 3:16.

Some worry about man "playing god," especially in matters of life and death. However, keeping someone alive to the bitter end would seem to involve "playing god" to a greater extent than letting nature take its course when interventions prove too costly and futile. Moreover, the real challenge is not to avoid playing god but to learn to play god well! Like a Near Eastern king giving an image of himself to his representative when sending him forth to do his business, the first biblical creation story portrays man as bearing God's image. [47] On this view, every person is God's vice-regent. Or, as St. Paul put it: We are ambassadors for Christ, God making his appeal through us. [48] Each of us is a product of the divine creativity, responsible for how we make use of the gifts with which we are endowed. To whom much is given, much is required, yet no one should bury his talents, however limited. [49] Everyone, women no less than men, should be afforded full exercise of creativity, power, and responsibility in work, politics, and family; to deny these to anyone is to dehumanize them. Man's essential being is "homo faber," man the fabricator of tools, arts, and ideas (Marx). A democratic politics, in which each citizen can vote and influence government, is a suitable institutionalization of divine empowerment. In the peroration of President Kennedy's inaugural address and in the prayer of Saint Francis, a readiness is expressed to be responsible agents and instruments of divine power: "Let us go forth to lead the land we love, asking for His blessing and His help, but knowing that here on earth God's work must truly be our own."

> Lord, make me an instrument of your peace:
> Where there is hatred, let me sow love;
> Where there is injury, pardon;
> Where there is doubt, faith;
> Where there is despair, hope;
> Where there is darkness, light;
> Where there is sadness, joy;
> O divine master,
> Grant that I may not so much seek to be consoled as to console;
> To be understood as to understand;
> To be loved as to love.
> For it is in giving that we receive.
> It is in pardoning that we are pardoned.
> It is in dying that we are born to eternal life.

---

[47] See Genesis 1:27.
[48] II Corinthians 5:20
[49] See Luke 12: 42-48; Matthew 25:14-30.

Although man may seem a puny creature in the vast universe, he is master of all he surveys on earth. Yet his mastery should not be misused to exploit the earth or fellow creatures or human kinfolk. Earth will last longer as a habitable planet if he takes good care of it as a faithful steward. If he keeps in touch with his humble earthly origins and treats the earth with gentleness, then future generations will have a beautiful earth to inherit. [50] Being in charge of animals, domesticated and wild, means exercising godly care for them.

> When I look at the heavens, the work of your fingers,
> the moon and the stars which you set set in their place,
> what is man that you are mindful of him,
> and the son of man that you care for him?
> Yet you have made him a little less than god
> and crowned him with glory and honor.
> You have set him in charge of all your creatures;
> You have put all of them under his feet:
> all sheep and oxen, all the wild animals,
> the birds of the air and the fish of the sea,
> even creatures that move along ocean paths. [51]

Man is made for mutuality. The tale is told of a primal human groundling (*adam*) who lived alone. He was blessed with animals as companions, whom he named, relating as many now with their pets-- dogs and cats and femurs and rats--but still he was lonely. Then he was blessed with the companionship of another human and shouted:

> This at last is bone of my bones
> and flesh of my flesh;
> She shall be called Woman (*ishah*)
> Because she was taken out of Man (*ish*). [52]

According to another tale, humans were originally two-sided: having two faces, four arms, four legs, two sets of privates, etc. Some were all male, some all female, some male on one side, female on the other. Having been split in two, each is forever seeking the other half. [53] Humans come from the same stock and are more alike than different. Those least encumbered by gender roles are the most happy.

---

[50] See Matthew 5:5. The meek shall inherit the earth.

[51] Psalm 8: 3-8.

[52] Genesis 2:23

[53] Drawn from Aristophanes' fable as discussed in Plato's <u>Symposium</u>.

Consonant with sexual differentiation in advanced species, most humans are male or female. Some, however, have a combination of male and female sexual organs; these are now called intersex persons. Most humans have a gender identity in tune with biological sex. Some, however, feel like they are females trapped in a male body or vice versa; these are transgendered persons. There is a sexual component in our natural love for ourselves and for our neighbors. Freud recognized an infantile sexuality encompassing the pleasure children as well as adults derive from touching ourselves and others, including erogenous zones. We are all naturally omnisexual, all of us investing a degree of libido in all of our significant relationships. In Freud's quaint phrase, we humans are "polymorphously perverse" since our sexual drives are not directed toward any specific object. Through interaction of natural inclination and cultural channeling, most humans are sexually attracted mainly to persons of opposite sex. Some, however, feel an almost exclusive sexual attraction to persons of the same sex or feel a degree of attraction to both sexes; these are gay, lesbian, and bisexual persons. Sexual activity with members of the same sex, especially males, is not uncommon among animals, including primates, so it cannot be considered "unnatural" though it more often expresses domination than mutuality for brutes. When we universalize the myth of our divine origins, we need to widen it to include not only Adam and Eve but also Adam and Steve as well as Madam and Eve. Regardless of sex, sexual orientation, or gender (or race or creed), all are God's creatures, children of God, made in God's image and empowered to be God's responsible agents. Gay, lesbian, bisexual, and transgendered persons should be accorded full civil rights in terms of employment, housing, protection, benefits, and family; many have their relationships solemnized as holy unions or recognized as domestic partnerships and are raising children from a continuing marriage, a former marriage, artificial insemination, or adoption. Persons of unusual sexual orientation may have special status in some cultures, such as the spiritually gifted *berdache* in native American cultures or affinity for the arts in western culture, but sexual orientation should not become a master status or stigma. Everyone should accept completely who he is in terms of orientation but express himself carefully, balancing the animal urges of the id and the cultural prescriptions of the superego and subjecting both to the norms of love and justice. Those who unite sexually become one flesh, whether in love or lust. Sex with a prostitute is likely to smack more of lust and exploitation than of love and justice. [54]

---

[54] See Gen. 2:24, I Cor. 6:15-16. See the Presbyterian report on sexuality, Keeping Body and Soul Together (1991: not adopted).

Mutuality plays itself out in a rhythm of union and separation. Union involves self-sacrifice for the whole, but too much union can foster domination and dependency. Separation involves self-growth, but too much separation breeds indifference and loneliness. There is a polarity between individualization and participation, such that the more the self is individualized the more it offers relationships, and the more one participates in relationships, the fuller the self. [55] Togetherness spiced with aloneness is the best recipe for harmony:

You were born together, and together you shall be forevermore
You shall be together
    when the white wings of death scatter your days.
But let there be spaces in your togetherness,
And let the winds of the heavens dance between you...
Love one another, but make not a bond of love;
Let it rather be a moving sea between your souls.
Sing and dance together and be joyous,
    but let each of you also be alone,
Even as the strings of a lute are alone
    though they quiver with the same music...
And stand together, yet not too near together;
For the pillars of the temple stand apart,
And the oak tree and the cypress grow
    not in each other's shadow. [56]

Besides ecstatic, rhapsodic union, there is sharing of larger purposes:

Were I to make of thee a statue of glittering glass
Annealed upon a pedestal of burnished brass,
Were I to place thee on the altar of my heart
And daily burn the incense of my spirit's art
In sweet, enchanted poetry and paeans of praise,
'Twere but a drear and fleshless sepulchre for thee I raise.

Were I to make of thee a woman and a wife
And make thy womb to be the bearer of my life,
Were I to place thee in the closeness of my home
And daily share with thee my burdens in the gloam,
We'd find in serving God and man through all out days
A life more fair than any temple hands can raise. [57]

---

55 See Paul Tillich, Systematic Theology, vol. I, pp. 174-178.

56 Kahlil Gibran, The Prophet, pp. 15-16. I use this (as cut) in weddings.

57 My poem to my wife: "To Susan"

Mutuality extends beyond the coupling pair (or affectional group or community) into responsibility for generations fore and aft. Everyone has parents and a responsibility to care for them in old age; it is part of honoring father and mother. In some cultures, marriages are neo-local so that newlyweds leave father and mother and cleave to each other; in others, parents and older relatives remain part of an extended household. There is a general human mandate, shared with all living creatures, to be fruitful and multiply and fill the earth though the process needs to slow down once the earth is filled. [58] It is quite possible to live a fulfilling life without fulfilling this mandate individually. Mutuality, including its sexual expression, does not exist just for the sake of procreation. Some marry and have no children; some do not marry. Jesus did not marry and considered his disciples rather than his relatives to be his family. Saint Paul thought it better not to marry in light of the urgency of the time in which he lived. [59] Whether married or not, all adults are called to generativity, producing work or children or both, and have a stake in raising the next generation. For those who marry, devotion to family must not be all-consuming but should be stretched to include wider circles, especially those without family. Pure religion is this: to help widows and orphans and to defang the domination system (*cosmos*). [60] Family members should not lord it over one another but bear one another's burdens with gentleness. There is no excuse for engaging in domestic violence or child abuse. Spouses and children are not property, and they have the right to their own self-expression. [61]

> Your children are not your children.
> They are the sons and daughters of Life's longing for itself.
> They come through you but not from you,
> And though they are with you yet they belong not to you.
> You may give them your love but not your thoughts.
> You may house their bodies but not their souls,
> For their souls dwell in the house of tomorrow...
> You are the bows from which your children as living arrows
>   are sent forth.
> The archer sees the mark upon the path of the infinite,
>   and He bends you with His might
>   that His arrows may go swift and far.

---

[58] See Genesis 2:24; Exodus 20:12; Genesis 1:28.
[59] See Mark 3:31-35; I Corinthians 7
[60] See Matthew 10:34-39; James 1:27.
[61] See Mark 10:35-45; Gal. 6:1-5; Kahlil Gibran, The Prophet, pp. 17-18.

Each of us in essentially a child of the divine though each of strays and loses touch with our divine roots. We come into this world, as it were, "trailing clouds of immortality (Wordsworth)." Although mortality and immorality are not essentially related, there comes in rather close proximity to both the child and the race the awareness of mortality and the dawn of moral consciousness. We realize that we are limited beings, neither immortal nor wholly good. We see that death is inevitable, we rue that we give ourselves over to death in killing others, and we fear death and its aftermath:

> Thou hideous spider weaving webs at night,
> Unfailing scourge of all mankind,
> Whose ruthless tentacles squeeze out the grume
> From victims in thy web entwined.
>
> Thy cruel, sanguinary instruments,
> Engrasped in man's inhuman claws
> Create the ghastly gore of battlefields
> And haste the closing of thy jaws.
>
> Grim guardian of dank dungeon depths,
> Thou endest mortal misery
> To make man witness horrors yet unknown
> Enshrined in frigid tombs by thee. [62]

Death comes not only at the end of life but invades our very being, which we come to understand as being toward death (Heidegger). Since death comes alike to man and beast, to the wise and the foolish, it may seem that all man's toil is vanity and a striving after wind. [63]

> Tomorrow and tomorrow and tomorrow
> Creeps in its petty pace from day to day,
> And all our yesterdays
> Have but lighted fools the way to dusty death.
> Out, out, brief candle.
> Life is but a passing shadow,
> A poor player who struts and frets
> His hour upon the stage and then is heard no more.
> It is a tale, told by an idiot, full of sound and fury,
> Signifying nothing.

---

[62] My poem, "Ode to Death," was printed in my high school literary magazine, white type on a black background superimposed on a white spider web.

[63] Ecclesiastes 1:14, 3:19; William Shakespeare, "MacBeth."

Death can diminish life not only though despair but also in defiance. The tale is told of a primeval couple who are expelled from paradise and made subject to death, toil, pain, and shame after they disobey God by falling for a snake's tempting promises that they will become immortal and can be like God knowing good and evil if they eat the apple he offers. [64] Although women and men did not bring death, toil, and pain into the world, awareness of these was at one time--for all and for each--a new experience and is tinctured by knowledge that human choice can hasten or lessen them. Movement from dreaming innocence to actualized freedom is experienced as gain as well as loss (Tillich). It is good that we come to make self-conscious choices and to weigh the consequences of our actions. Although the dawn of moral consciousness brings with it some sense of good and evil, this sense is mainly a parental and cultural residue; even if we think things through for ourselves, we can never have full divine knowledge of morality any more than we can be immortal. Yet the benighted quest continues. Not accepting our limitations, we further limit ourselves. Not accepting ourselves as we are, in shame, we cover our nakedness with pretense. The impulse to be immortal, timeless, and perfect renders us self-centered, self-righteous, proud, cutting us off from the divine, fellow humans, and our true selves. We all have missed the mark and fallen short of our potential as limited human beings, exchanging our divinely ordained glory for vainglory. [65] Estranged from the ground of our being, we become insecure about our selves, seek to protect, wall off, and aggrandize our selves, draw back from self-giving love, and make our selves less than we could be. We fall down when we do not live up to love. We become murderous, forget that we are our brother's keeper, enslave our brothers, forget the forbearance signified by the rainbow along with the diversity of languages and cultures which are our heritage as we babel on without understanding each other. [66] If we approach our shortcomings by condemning ourselves as sinners or excusing ourselves as sick, we dig the pit deeper. Only if we open ourselves to reunion with the ground of our being and growing into our potential do we stand a chance of becoming fully human; we cannot overcome evil with evil, including disparagement, but only with good. [67]

---

[64] See Genesis 3.

[65] See Romans 3:23. *Amartia*, often translated as "sin," comes from archery and literally means missing the target. See also Psalm 8:5.

[66] See Genesis 4, 9, 11.

[67] Growth is a better frame for therapy than sin or sickness, according to Virginia Satir, Conjoint Family Therapy, 181-183. See Romans 12:21.

In the earliest religions we know there is a sense of paradise lost and of the "immemorial misdirection" of life. The ancestors did everything first and did it in an exemplary manner, serving as pioneers of occupations and progenitors of clans, nations, races. [68] In the primitive view, we stray when we lose touch with the ancestors and with the ancestral ways, so we seek repeatedly to do things as they did and to renew our bonds with them. For the Navajo, sickness stems from isolation; they do not seek to isolate the sick, as moderns do, but to restore community. The Navajo Sing begins with sweating and vomiting to expel the sickness, moves to visitation by the whole tribe to sing their well wishes, and culminates in laying the sick person down upon a sand painting of the holy people of yore so that his or her weakness might be exchanged for their strength. Among the aborigines of Australia, untouched by neolithic culture, each clan identifies itself with a different totem animal, for which it is named. The totem is not a "god" and is not "worshiped," for the totem is not different from them and has no special "worthship." Rather the totem is themselves writ large, an emblem of the clan. It is their sacred essence, reflected in the totem animal and in each and every clan member. When they are dispersed and engaged in the several mundane tasks of daily living, they can lose sight of their essence, but when they all gather together in sacred ceremony, they revive who they really are. The totem animal, too sacred to kill under ordinary circumstances, is now killed and eaten, restoring their essence. Their identification with the totem is renewed through retelling ancient stories, impersonating mythic figures, human and animal, reenacting archetypal events, singing, dancing, and shouting. In the "everywhen" of collective ritual, all time barriers dissolve allowing ancestors to be present, and all barriers between persons melt as the clan achieves complete unity. The individual with all his deficiencies is offered up, destroyed, transformed, and returned whole in communion with the clan as a whole, living and returned. In the Corrobbori, there is great excitement, ecstasy, and excess. In the collective effervescence, the expressed sentiments of one are reechoed by the next as a sort of electricity passes through the clan transporting them to an extraordinary degree of exaltation. Passions burst out in violent gestures, cries, howls, singing and dancing, and even in extramarital and incestuous sex, surpassing the usual rules, as the ritual reaches a fever pitch in darkness pierced by firelight. [69]

---

68 See Genesis 4: 17-22 plus the many genealogies in the Bible.
69 See Emile Durkheim, Elementary Forms of the Religious Life, pp. 246-248 and Robert Bellah, "Religious Evolution," in Beyond Belief, pp. 23-29.

In looking for parallels in contemporary life, it has been noted that cheering crowds at football games and rock concerts comport much more with the spirit of primal religious ceremony than do prim and proper attendees at tepid church services listening to wordiness and singing without passion hymns left over from previous centuries. Something elemental is missing. Saturday at "Phantom of the Opera" I was enthralled by the dark passions and inspiring genius of the angel of music, released at last from ugliness by a redemptive kiss, but Sunday I sat upon the pew basically uninvolved. Moderns gain release through tawdry drugs and sex and drunkenness or swooning before pop idols or devotion to sports teams which represent us, but rarely are we caught up in something larger than ourselves. An exception was the murder and funeral of President John Kennedy:

> This was a ritualized occasion of the greatest social necessity. The public murder of a president, representing our whole society, the living social organism of which we ourselves were the members, taken away at a moment of exuberant life, required a compensatory rite to reestablish the sense of solidarity. Here was an enormous nation, made those four days into a unanimous community, all of us participating in the same way, simultaneously, in a single symbolic event. [70]

There are vestiges of a totemic feast in Christian communion, some openness to ecstatic utterance in Pentecostal churches, some hint of the ghosts of dead ancestors roaming our world at Halloween, a taste of unbridled collective exuberance in Mardi Gras or a Mexican fiesta. But we are generally long on theology and short on experience. After seeing lots of shrines and ceremonies, an American asked a Japanese shinto priest about shinto ideology and theology; the priest replied: "I think we don't have ideology. We don't have theology. We dance." If we are to meet God in our time, perhaps we must encounter him in the dance before we can define him in the doctrine.[71] Perhaps the form that our theology needs to take is a song of faith. Some primal strains--but not primal screams--can be worked into our singing. Although primitive society is too stifling and tradition-bound to provide a direct model for us, we would do well to acknowledge our debt to our ancestral society in terms of art, language, and culture and to provide more nourishment for our elementary religious needs.

---

[70] Joseph Campbell, The Power of Myth, p. xiv (recalled by Bill Moyers). See also my PhD thesis, The Kennedy Myth: American Civil Religion in the 60s.

[71] Campbell, op. cit., p. xix. See Harvey Cox, Feast of Fools, p. 28.

Another area where we can learn from the primitives is in our approach to nature. Although the disenchantment of nature as part of secularization has been a boon to humankind in terms of making science and its benefits possible, we tend to disparage our bodies and to lose track of our connection to the earth and to other creatures. Native Americans challenge us to own less and to relate more: [72]

How can you buy the sky?
How can you own the rain and the wind?
Every part of this earth is sacred to our people.
Every pine needle. Every shady shore.
Every mist in the dark woods.
Every meadow and humming insect.
All are holy in the memory of our people.
We are part of the earth and it is part of us.
The perfumed flowers are our sisters.
The bear, the deer, the great eagle, these are our brothers.
The rocky crests, the meadows, the ponies--
    all belong to the same family.
Each ghostly reflection in the clear waters of the lakes tells
    of memories in the life of our people.
The water's murmur is the voice of your great-great-grandmother.
You must keep the land and air apart and sacred,
    as a place where one can go taste the wind that
    is sweetened by the meadow flowers...
This we know: All things are connected like the blood that unites us.
We did not weave the web of life,
We are merely a strand in it.
Whatever we do to the web, we do to ourselves.
We love this earth as a newborn loves its mother's heartbeat.
If we sell you our land, care for it as we have cared for it.
Hold in your mind the memory of the land
    as it is when you receive it.
Preserve the land and the air and the rivers for your
    children's children and love it as we have loved it.
Every part of this soil is sacred in the estimation of my people.
Every hillside, every valley, every plain and grove, has been
    hallowed by some sad or happy event in days long vanished.
Even the rocks which seem to be dumb and dead
    as they swelter in the sun along the silent shore,
    thrill with memories of stirring events connected with my people.

---

72 Attributed to Chief Seattle in Susan Jeffers' Brother Eagle, Sister Sky.

The sense of the sacredness of all things is something that we need to recover from our late-primitive ancestors and contemporary cousins. As tribes replace clans as the basis of social organization, the totemic principle is no longer represented by a single totem but by a set of totems (as on the totem pole) or in more diverse forms. As settled agriculture plus hunting or herding replaces nomadic hunting and gathering, attachment to particular features of the environment as sacred increases, especially to land in which the bones of ancestors is buried. As the collective leadership of elders in politics and religion is supplemented by specialized chiefs and shamans, these figures are invested with special sacredness and are expected to mediate sacredness to the people: with chiefs, after consultation with elders, setting the sacred course for the tribe and shamans, after visions, elaborating on the fluid traditional theology. What emerges from these developments is a commendable notion of divine energy--called <u>mana</u> by the Melanesians, <u>wakan</u> by the Sioux, <u>orenda</u> by the Iroquois--cropping up everywhere but in different measures: in animals and ancestors and tribesmen as always, in chiefs and shamans in extra measure as expected and in unexpected feats of prowess in hunting or war or uncanny experiences of vision, possession, or healing, in familiar features of the environment and in special measure in burial mounds and in titanic displays of nature. Life is wonderful--and terrible--for the primitive as he encounters the holy in ordinary and extraordinary circumstances, as *mysterium tremens et fascinans* (Rudolph Otto). It is here that religion is born and then encapsulated in myth and ritual. At worst the world is seen as spooky and many rituals need to be repeated (religion as *relegere*) to appease capricious spirits, as with ancient Roman numen or shinto kami. At best folk bind themselves to each other (religion as *religare*) as they seek to restore their essential being.

Primal religion is thoroughly corporate at the core but also individualized at the edges. When his time comes, an aboriginal Australian lad goes off alone into the wilderness on his walkabout, and through this ordeal and deprivation and accompanying visions, he becomes a man. Likewise, the shaman lives at the edges of life and so can help those who are *in extremis,* such as the sick, whom he may aid with herbal medicine (whence the misnomers "medicine man" or "witch doctor"). In some tribes the shaman is a *berdache,* a gay or bisexual man seen as blessed with both a male and female spirit and thus better able to counsel with both men and women. Suffering more than most, the shaman is wizened by his ordeals and prone to visions.

In his great vision, Black Elk encounters powers, who are both separate and one Power, clothed in imagery at once ancestral and natural and divine. After being sick, he feels himself swept up on a cloud into the sky at the calling of his six Grandfathers in council. The first Grandfather bestows his spirit and gives him a cup of water to make live and a bow to destroy before turning into a black horse and heading off to the West, where the sun goes down and thunder beings live. The second Grandfather gives him an herb and a white wing to cleanse before turning into a white goose wheeling North. The third Grandfather gives him a peace pipe to heal, and soon fat bison galloped to the East. The fourth Grandfather gave him a holy tree to center the people's life and encourage growth and then ran as an elk toward the South. The fifth Grandfather, the Spirit of the Sky, gave him the power of winds and stars and became a hovering eagle. The sixth Grandfather, the Spirit of the Earth, was himself grown old. All of the grandfathers addressed him as a younger brother and promised him their powers. But the vision included seeing the sad ordeal of his people as the holy tree was destroyed and the nation's hoop was broken. In desperation Black Elk turned with others to the lesser vision of the Payute messiah Wovoka, who prophesied that a new world would descend from heaven crushing the white man and leaving only Native Americans, living and revived, alive. They drew upon ancestral power in their "ghost dances", but their ghost shirts, far from invincible, were no shield against the white man's bullets. [73]

Before they were done in by superior firepower and infernal firewater, decimated by unfamiliar diseases (some from virus-laden blankets) and forced marches, sidelined by scientific progress and an alien civilization, disheartened by failed magic and abject poverty, the American Indians, like other traditional peoples around the globe struggling for survival in a hostile environment, relied upon their ancestral religion to seek attunement with nature and access to her powers. The purpose of this primal religion was to make this world run right. The revival of vegetation in the spring and the birthing of the next generation of animals was a prime concern, which required ceremonial sympathetic magic by humans to insure and inspire. Man and nature lived in interdependence. Nature feeds man with harvest when nature is strong while man scatters pulverized sacred rock dust or chewed yams or ground seeds or water or his own blood to help growth return again when nature is weak and dormant. [74]

---

73 Black Elk Speaks (ed. John G. Niehardt), pp. 17-25, 31-32, 195-198, 211-230.

74 See Emile Durkheim, Elementary Forms of the Religious Life, pp. 368-374.

This religion of the countryside can be called paganism and its wisdom wicca. It is the "elementary form" of religion, the root of all religions, even those which later turn against it. It is the fertility religion of the Canaanites in which men copulating with ritual prostitutes were believed to inspire the husbands of the land (baals) to impregnate her. Leaders of the Israelites repudiated this religion again and again since it persisted in ceremonies "under every green tree" and even insinuated itself into the palace, as when King Saul visited the witch of Endor or when King Ahab imported foreign equivalents under the domination of his infamous queen Jezebel. Paganism has also persisted within and alongside Christianity over the centuries and has taken a new lease on life in contemporary neo-paganism. The names for our lesser divisions of time reflect our pagan heritage. Days are named for the great orbs in our sky, Sun and Moon, for the Roman god of bounty, Saturn, and for Teutonic and Norse gods. Some months are named for Roman gods: Janus, Mars, Juno. Paganism also persists in a seasonal calendar including such holidays (holy days) as halloween, yule, new year, carnival, easter, fool's day, and May Day. In Europe, they still carry out straw effigy of Death, beat him, spread the straw on fields, and celebrate the May, with the maypole as tree bedecked, a phallic pole with vaginal ribbons. Here is what they say when bringing in summer:

> We have carried Death out,
> We are bringing the dear Summer back,
> The Summer and the May
> And all the flowers gay.[75]

It is as if Spring has come to life again after a winter of being dead. The ancient Greeks tell a tale of a maiden Persephone, who, romping gaily in the meadow, falls through a cleft in the earth to the underworld, presided over by Hades. He invites her in to his table, but once she has tasted a morsel of his food, she is bound to stay. Her mother Demeter, a goddess of grain, is distraught as vegetation dies in the absence of the spring goddess, and weeps inconsolably. Finally, Hades relents and lets Persephone work her magic on earth for most of the year but takes her back each winter.

We appreciate spring more when it bursts forth in beauty in climes where it is not perpetual. We celebrate the rebirth of vegetation, its flowering, and its demise as seasons come and go, and we revel in the birth and growth of animals in the various seasons of life:

---

[75] Sir James Frazier, <u>The Golden Bough,</u> p. 362.

The leaf begins its cycle soft
And small and green and delicate.
The snow takes shape in realms aloft,
Each flake without a duplicate.
The bird emerges sheathed in down
And chirps its cry for sustenance.
The horse comes forth besmirched and brown;
On shaky legs it starts to dance.

The leaf in red and gold expires.
The snow on fir our joy inspires.
The bird will sport its plumage bright.
The horse will leap as if in flight,
A world of beauty waits us 'round.
Its source of zest in change is found.[76]

The joy of summer is easily treasured as is the cornucopia of harvest
and the resplendent colors of autumn, but winter has its lure as well:

Winter is here:
The time of crackling fires
And burnished andirons
In the old stone fireplace,
Of rocking and knitting
In the dim firelight,
Of reading gay novels
Filled with adventures
Of silvered knights
And scarlet queens.

Winter is here:
The time when nature takes pause
From her feverish toil
To sleep beneath a blanket
Of soft, cool snow,
The time this world of white
Stops to sing the old carols
Commemorating birth
And then, reborn,
Sings in new life
With a new year.[77]

---

76 My poem "Change"
77 My poem "Winter"

In the winter solstice celebration, we long for the light and life that emerges out of darkness:

> Blessed is the darkness,
> For in the darkness we conceive.
> Blessed is the light,
> For in light we give birth.[78]

We commit ourselves to emerge into the full glory of our potential and to inspire others to join with us:

> Our deepest fear is not that we are inadequate.
> Our deepest fear is that we are powerful beyond measure.
> It is our light, not our darkness, that most frightens us.
> We ask ourselves, who am I to be brilliant,
> gorgeous, talented, and fabulous?
>
> Actually, who are you *not* to be?
>
> You are a child of God.
> Your playing small does not serve the world.
> There's nothing enlightened about shrinking
> so that other people won't feel insecure around you.
>
> We were born to make manifest
> the glory of God that is within us.
> It's not just in some of us; it's in everyone.
>
> And as we let our own light shine,
> we unconsciously give other people permission to do the same.
>
> As we are liberated from our own fear,
> Our presence automatically liberates others.[79]

What I affirm in the ancient wisdom (wicca) is: the love of nature, the sense of wonder, the feeling of the rhythm of the seasons as we celebrate their passage, and the positive appreciation of sensuality and sexuality, fertility, pleasure, and beauty. Power earthly and celestial is imaged as female and male, mother earth and father sky, the moon and the sun. We bask in their light and love:

---

[78] "A Winter Solstice Singing Ritual," p. 17.
[79] Marianne Williamson, "A Return to Love" in "A Winter Solstice Singing Ritual," p. 40.

And you who reach for the stars in the heavens,
Turning your back on the fields that you've sowed,
Still live in the light of the Lord and the Lady.
The greater the circle, the more their love grows.

This is the charge of the Goddess: "All acts of love and pleasure are My rituals." "Do no harm" is the watchword of wizards and witches. Though humans are called to more, it is wonderful when they share pleasure lovingly and harmlessly. It is perfectly normal and natural. All actual entities seek enjoyment (Whitehead). Carnal love as well as sacrificial love exhibits the divine. As a Taize chant puts it: "Ubi caritas et amor, ubi caritas, dues ibi est." Where there is charitable love and amorous love, wherever there is love, there is God.

It is a mistake to denigrate amorous love in favor of charitable love in the guise of flesh versus spirit. Flesh and spirit are not physical and mental but have to do with orientation away from or toward the divine. The Gospel of John exclaims that the Word became flesh. I cannot conceive of Jesus being conceived other than by intercourse, and Jesus may have married before embarking on ministry at age 30. There is no warrant for an all-male celibate priesthood. Having such a priesthood is privative, psychologically unhealthy, and hard to staff. Although the disciples were portrayed as twelve men to represent twelve tribes of Israel, women were among Jesus' followers and should be among his priests. So should gays. Marriage and holy unions should not be denied to priests, monks, and nuns.

A monk and a nun in the still of the night
Stole into the chapel where vespers had been.
Silently praying, they kneel on the velveteen
Carpet before the high altar. The nun's white
Face half-glows in the soft, tinted moonlight,
While her hand she hides in his, unseen.
Filled with passion, they kneel, so pure and serene;
Their crosses clink as their lips unite.

Fill my cup with holy love,
O God, sweetened with a warm embrace.
Give me Thy mountains and a pleasant grove
And a clear, swift brook for my dwelling-place.
Make me a clean heart with Thy winds from above,
So I may see her in the light of Thy face.[80]

---

80 My poem "Sonnet on Holy Love"

A newborn baby cries and is fed. Hunger and eating, pain and pleasure, is the basic rhythm for babies and all humans, rounded out by activity and rest. Meeting a baby's need for food, comfort, cuddling, and sleep is the heart of mother love. There is no finer love; it is divine love. The table grace, which I grew up saying, exclaimed:

> God is great and God is good.
> Now we thank him for our food.
> By thy hands may all be fed.
> Give us, Lord, our daily bread.

Though earth is rife with divine bounty, God has no hands but ours. We need to provide basic nutrition, sanitation, and health care for all. Babies are fed and cured without having to deserve or earn it, and in our global plenteous world this can and should be true for everyone. Eating is pleasant and good though too much gluttony is a waste and a drag and can lead to morbid obesity. The balance of hunger and food outweighs instant gratification and perpetual satiation or starvation. When the nipple on breast or bottle comes in time in love, the infant finds its universe to be trustworthy and develops a primal faith. Receiving love and expressing trust is the infant's joy. The heavenly kingdom is accessible only to those with attitudes of little children. No matter how old we get, we should listen to our inner child. A sense of awe and wonder and of playfulness is never to be outgrown.

As a child grows, activity time increases and sleep time diminishes. Mobility develops, and senses become more acute. Playing without accomplishment is common: the blocks are built and knocked down. Meaning is in the process, not in the result. The child is socialized, learning to speak language, to interact with others and respond to their feelings, and to take account of externally imposed rules, whose violation can bring shame. The natural pressure for release is tamed into habits of cleanliness through patient toilet training. Willfulness often emerges during the "terrible twos," but the trick is not to break the spirit of the child but to foster a robust though limited autonomy.

Horizons of the preschool child are wildly expanded if encouraged. Everything is open to curiosity and exploration including erogenous zones. Imagination takes flight, and fantasy life is rich. Children play house and play doctor anticipating grown-up roles. Parental and social rules are internalized into conscience with attendant guilt. It is best not to overdo guilt, which is a disabling emotion; those who are preoccupied with sin are sinners (Joseph Campbell). Rather the aim should be to encourage initiative within appropriate boundaries.

Schooling can give a major boost to a child's lifelong adventure in learning. Education at all levels improves life chances, and nothing is more effective in stemming rapid population growth than education of women for jobs outside the home. Education should be available to all on the basis of merit, and the potential of every child should be developed equitably in terms of academic, athletic, and artistic gifts. The emotionality of the preschool years wanes for the school child, and a tamer friendship among buddies, pals, and teammates emerges, more often than not boys with boys and girls with girls. The intuitive and projective faith of the fantasy-prone gives way to a mythic-literal approach where stories, religious and otherwise, are gobbled up but with little discernment. Industrious habits can be cultivated, and if grading is not too degrading and competition not overly intense, a sense of competence and a feeling of self-esteem will be fostered.

Children are naturally self-centered and selfish, and there is nothing wrong with that. A growing understanding will enable a morality of instrumental hedonism, in which pleasure is sought and pain avoided, not just immediately but in the long run. It is important for a child to have self-love, for self-love is the source from which all loving comes, including embracing divine love and loving neighbor as one's self. Even Jesus took time for himself and loved eating and drinking so much he was tagged as a glutton and a wino. He practiced an open table fellowship in which everyone was welcomed with conviviality. There is a problem with self-love only if it does not expand. The childish attitude that says "Screw everybody else; I want mine," which advertising encourages in a consumerist culture, is pernicious. No wonder that global warming increases each year as we are unwilling to curb self-indulgence in favor of the simpler lifestyle required for sustainability. Instrumental hedonism would indicate the folly of fouling our own nests though it is best to go beyond such hedonism.

We are on the downward side from the peak of having used up half of the planet's oil, and the burning of petroleum derivatives and other fossil fuels has increased the carbon dioxide in the atmosphere to such an extent that trapped heat is warming the earth, resulting in melting glaciers near the poles and a rise in the level of the oceans and the expanding of tropical zones and of tropical diseases and an increase in the number and severity of hurricanes. Trees absorb CO_2 and could stem global warming some, but deforestation rooted in population pressure has increased, including decimation of tropical rain forests. Suburban sprawl and reliance on private automobiles wastes oil and increases pollution. We need to model and teach our children an ecological consciousness and a planetary ethic.

What comes after childhood? It used to be adulthood. The ancients had rites of passage. Yesterday you were a child; today you are a man. In aboriginal Australia, now as then, as bullroarers whirred loudly, the penis was cut in painful circumcision and the initiate was doused in the blood of men, born not as at first of woman but born again their fathers' sons. For girls it was not so much ritual as biology that made them women at their first menstruation.

But in contemporary American and other post-industrial societies, prolonged adolescence intervenes between childhood and adulthood. It begins with puberty, if not before, and extends indefinitely. Does a youth become adult when he or she gets a driver's license or a job, when the army makes a man of him, when drinking or voting are legal, when intercourse or wedding or parenting occur? It's not clear. There is much identity diffusion but also a golden opportunity to forge one's own identity over time as one grows intellectually and sexually and religiously. In Hinduism this is the stage of the student, typically accompanied by an orientation to pleasure. Adolescents are often both jaded and sheltered, having lost the innocence of a child in our sex-saturated culture but lacking adult experience as they grow up in suburban enclaves without racial or class diversity.

Religious communities attempt to ritualize this transition. For Jews there is a sense of passage from boys to men around puberty in the bar mitzvah for males (and bat mitzvah for females). For Baptists and their ilk, there is "believer's baptism," often at an age too young for passage, and a stress on being born again, which is reenacted publicly in burying the old self beneath the water and rising to newness of life. The experience of regeneration is usually too stereotyped, expected child of altar call and summer camp and sawdust trail, born of social pressure more than mystic flight. Conversion may hew too closely to Saul's upon the Damascus Road and yet the need for a major turning is rightly upheld. Catholics and mainline Protestants practice infant baptism but also have youth confirm their baptism, a transition only to or within adolescence.

> Children were they not before the call
> Nor are men thereafter but still boys
> Unaccustomed to the bullroar's noise:
> No ordeal, no blood, no water's fall.
> Unregenerate, forever Saul,
> No great light, no spear, no nuptial joys,
> Playing sports and driving cars as toys,
> Grown up only dressing at the mall.

We fill your heads with scads of information,
Require assent to doctrine not to life.
We leave your heart unscathed by reformation;
We shield your soul from agony and strife.
To be a man still waits for confirmation.
It's years before we let you take to wife.[81]

Confirmation of baptism could be much richer than it usually is. Rather than using classes leading to confirmation to stuff the tenets of a synthetic-conventional faith into young minds, students could be encouraged to begin the process of developing an individuative-reflexive faith. Adolescence is a natural time to doubt received stories and doctrines and to winnow the wheat from the chaff in critical thinking. Students should be encouraged to forge a faith of their own, spiced with insights from all the world's religions, rather than mindlessly adopting the faith of their fathers and mothers.

Like Jesus' baptism, baptism or its confirmation could be chrismation (being anointed to a mission: added to Eastern Orthodox baptism), commissioning to become a disciple of Jesus, ordination to ministry for every Christian, induction into service as a soldier for Christ, prepared for a life of hardship and sacrifice (once symbolized during a confirmation rite by a slap from a Catholic bishop), admission into the church militant, receiving apprenticeship training for disciplined leadership in acts of mercy and struggles for justice and peace.

After Jesus was baptized, he went into the wilderness for more than a month to be tested, and through that process he emerged again with his mission clarified. In aboriginal Australia, a lad may go into the wilderness for a few months without provisions on his "walkabout" learning self-reliance and discovering his own personal totem in addition to the clan totem. American culture, especially in suburban mode, is not of this cast. Aloneness is not prized but disparaged as loneliness; "loner" and "loser" differ by only one letter in our lexicon. There is enough individualism to undermine genuine community but plenty of conformity nonetheless. By contrast, young disciples could be encouraged to individuate themselves by adopting a sacrificial life, where risks are taken and challenges faced, where evil is confronted and encompassed and overcome, and to participate in community efforts to alleviate pain. Church work camps can expose teens to new people and environments even as they provide an avenue for service. Adolescents should learn to be world-serving as well as self-serving.

---

[81] My poem "Confirmation"

The influence of peers reaches its zenith among adolescents. Beyond style and fitting in, this portends a growth beyond hedonism into interpersonal concord, where needs and feelings of others are taken into account. Especially for some women in caregiver roles, this is their highest moral stage construing responsibility as responsiveness.

In dating and mating, intimacy deepens accompanied by tenderness and responsibility, a desire to please and be pleased, hedged by a commitment to avoid exploitation and do no harm. The archetypal energy of the Lover, a sensual and sexual energy, bursts forth in savoring sensation and in erotic love. This aspect of life is celebrated in the lingams and tantric yoga of Hinduism, but is suppressed in the West. The Quranic injunction to hide the bosom is often stretched to nearly total coverage. Not at all puritanical, Jesus welcomed his beloved disciple laying his head on his breast and the hospitable caresses of the woman of the streets. One can imagine him lying in the arms of Mary Magdalene as she sings "Let the world turn without you tonight" as in "Jesus Christ Superstar." Song of Songs exclaims:

Like an apricot tree among the trees of the wood,
So is my beloved among boys.
To sit in its shadow was my delight,
And its fruit was sweet to my taste.
He took me into the wine garden and gave me loving glances.
He refreshed me with raisins, he revived me with apricots,
For I was faint with love.
His left arm was under my head, his right arm was round me.

How beautiful are your sandaled feet, O prince's daughter.
The curves of your thighs are like jewels,
The work of a skilled craftsman.
Your navel is a rounded goblet
that never shall want for spiced wine.
Your belly is a heap of wheat fenced in by lilies.
You are stately as a palm tree,
And your breasts are the clusters of dates.
I said, 'I will climb up into the palm to grasp its fronds.'
May I find your breasts like clusters of grapes on the vine,
The scent of your breath like apricots,
And your whispers like spiced wine
Flowing smoothly to welcome my caresses
Gliding down through lips and teeth.[82]

[82] Song of Songs 2:3-6; 7:1-2, 7-9 (NEB). Formerly known as Song of Solomon.

Adulthood features generativity, production and reproduction, making work and making babies. In Hinduism this is the householder stage with the aim of success. The archetypal energy of the Warrior manifests itself in taking charge, maintaining discipline, withstanding ordeals courageously, and getting things done, preferably peacefully. Morality is often marked by a concern for Law and Order obeying existing laws and raising law-abiding children.

By mid-life, cracks may appear in the structured insularity of young adulthood. Single-minded devotion to monetary and occupational success, to what William James called the bitch goddess Success, so common in America and so definitive of the "American Dream," may come up wanting. As work becomes less engaging and the immediate family's need for care abates, adults in middle age, according to Hinduism, may widen the arena of their concern and do civic duty. The archetypal energy of the King reaches out in ordering and encouragement and blessing. Seeing gaps in current practice, the activist is more committed to the Social Contract by which better laws are made than to the laws on the books. Simple affirmations are rendered more complicated in a paradoxical/consolidative faith that holds opposing views in tension and seeks a unity behind them:

An organic unity,
A harmony of opposites
A melody of positive and negative,
A delight with the play of our vibratory existence.
When the opposites are realized to be one,
Discord melts into concord,
Battles become dances,
And old enemies become lovers.[83]

Old age can bring integrity, looking back at one's life as a whole and seeing it as whole. In Hinduism, this is the stage for detachment and fullness of being. The archetypal energy of the Magician draws on the wisdom of the ages and the aged as wizard and elder and sees deeply. Oldsters may push through to universal principles behind all morality, articulating a commitment to life and love in all situations. A universalizing faith is possible in which symbols from many traditions become luminous, all being is embraced, and love, which colors every stage, is most fully actualized.[84]

---

83 Ken Wilber, <u>No Boundary,</u> p. 29.

84 Psychosocial stages come from Erik Erikson, moral stages from Lawrence Kohlberg, faith stages from Jim Fowler, and archetypes from Carl Gustav Jung.

Lost in the mists of time is my childhood. I must have been well nourished and cared for, for I trust the universe and trust other people. Toilet training seems to have left no scars, for I have habits of cleanliness without being averse to dirt. I follow most of the rules but have always been adventuresome. When my mother attached my clothes to a clothesline, I escaped from my clothing and was found naked near a busy street. When I knew better but ventured beyond where I was allowed in order to visit a haunted estate, I nearly drowned in a pond, but luckily someone found a rope and pulled me in to safety. I have always been industrious winning a contest in first grade for reading the most books and presenting a report over three days in sixth grade.

Adolescence was a placid period for me. I took confirmation classes and became a member of the liberal Presbyterian church in which my parents were active, and I became president of the youth fellowship. But my real god was achievement. In a seventh-grade psychology book I read that our three needs are affection, acceptance, and achievement. I figured I received sufficient affection at home, had minimal acceptance since I did not see myself as popular, but could really shine in achievement. I always did well at school, and a fellow brain and I were voted "most likely to succeed" in our senior year. I took part in plays and sang in three choirs: at school, at Presbyterian church, and at the Catholic church since I liked to sing in Latin. I was a latecomer to sports since I was so inept as a child at baseball, basketball, and football. I did not know that running was a sport, but since I was, literally, "always running late" to school, I got plenty of practice. I excelled as a track star. Although my greatest achievement was running the mile in 4 minutes and 43 seconds, I was most celebratory when I ran a quarter mile in less than a minute giving joint credit to God and myself:

Thank you, God of the grey-white sky,
Thanks for the quarter in fifty-nine,
Thanks for the guts to breeze right by
The starting and the finish line.

Thanks for the strength throughout the race,
Thanks for the joy of victory mine,
For the arms and legs and teeth-clenched face
That brought me the quarter in fifty-nine.[85]

---

[85] My poem "A Runner's Prayer"

A crisis arose when I discovered that the country cross-country meet and state chorus concert were on the same day. I could not do both. The glory of one achievement or the other would be lacking, and I would have to let down either my athletic coach or my choir director. After much agonizing, I chose the cross-country meet, where I was an irreplaceable part of a team, over the state chorus, where I could be and was replaced by a boy from Bayonne. My achievement god had failed, and I would never again place so much credence in Success.

As a freshman at Oberlin College I was attracted to the Inter-Varsity Christian Fellowship. They put a great deal more emphasis on conversion and commitment than I was used to. In conjunction with a conference in Pittsburgh, after hearing testimony from a seamstress on a bus, I dedicated my life to God, whoever He might be. It stuck. Though I soon enough found the certitude and fixed smiles of the Inter-Varsity folks to be cloying, my faith and purpose have remained relatively constant even as my beliefs have changed considerably.

A philosophy professor at Oberlin told me that I could not really do philosophy since I accepted religion as a given. Yet I am sure I doubted my religion at least as much as he questioned his irreligion. I always walk in the borderland between religion and irreligion. This did not make it easy for me to get under the care of presbytery as a candidate for ministry. Some members of the Candidates Committee expected me to have had a conversion experience akin to that of St. Paul on the road to Damascus, and were appalled that I could make no claim to a direct call from God to ministry. For me it was indirect. As a kid, I was impressed by an uncle who was a medical missionary, and I wanted to be of service in a way like that though I did not want to give people shots since they hurt so much. Now that I had a fairly firm identity in terms of basic faith and vocational aspiration, I figured that I had developed the God-given talents and interests that suited me for ministry in a church that could use some reformation in theological thought and worldly action. I was accepted as a candidate at a second appearance, perhaps because my home pastor construed my remarks as reflecting "the critical love of the church."

Intimacy has always come easily to me. I have never met a stranger. Inspired by the image of an all-inclusive God who showers the world with rain and grace, I readily share my affection with family and friends. I love myself, and I love my neighbors; I am a love machine. As a young adult, I dated a little, fell in love, married, and raised two sons in a loving home. Yet my love was not bounded by family. I also fancied myself as a playful vagabond and rover.

A homeless sylph, I wander endless miles.
A vagabond am I, a gypsy rover.
I sleep tonight with Todd, tomorrow Grover.
A playful sprite, I exercise my wiles
To gain safe berth and bed me down with smiles.
Where blows the wind, where sweetly smells the clover,
Just waft a scented breeze, and I'll buzz over,
A dancing bee whom beauty's beast beguiles.

I seek a home, a place to settle down,
To rest my weary bones. My heart will sing
The joys of married life. And yet the clown
In me grows restless. Like a hawk with wing
Outstretched, I yearn to fly, to paint the town,
To give my untamed self a final fling.[86]

As an adult, I have expressed generativity not only in producing and raising a family but also in pursuing ideas and activities energetically. I have a B.A. in Philosophy from Oberlin College in Ohio, an M.Div. in theology from Union Theological Seminary in New York , and a PhD in Religion and Society from Graduate Theological Union in Berkeley (plus a B.S. and an M.S. in Computer Science). I worked three years with a black church in Cleveland's inner city, taught religious studies and sociology for a decade in Canada and Iowa, taught computer science for five at IU East in Richmond, and was a programmer at Golden Rule Insurance in Indianapolis for 15 years, during and after which I have been an adjunct professor at local universities, including IUPUI, Butler, and University of Indianapolis. I am still going strong with my teaching and community involvement. I am president of the Indianapolis Peace and Justice Center and convener of Common Bonds, an umbrella for progressive groups, under whose aegis I send out a weekly email to 2000 people telling them what is going on in Indy and around the state in terms of peace, justice, labor, race, gay rights, women's rights, and environment. To such causes I have devoted my life.

My approach is praxis, where ideas and activities are melded, with another component as well: Exposure, Reflection, and Action (ERA). It might not have been so. I loved philosophical discussion in college and considered becoming a Greek professor in the ivory tower. But the activist side of me prevailed over the monkish.

---

[86] My poem "Wild"

I can feel the world
Breathing down my back.
I can hear her savage cries
For food, for truth, for love.
I can see her turgid misery,
Her calloused outstretched hands...

And yet I try to close myself
Within these four pink walls,
To blind myself and laugh
In my hollow, bloodless sanctuary,
To speak to none but God
In His cold, celestial solitude.

But the earth-people calls
And the living God commands.
I can no longer sit alone;
I shall come to my people.
I shall come with the fire of lightning
And the strength of a mighty river.[87]

The struggle for civil rights engaged much of my sense of mission. Growing up in a suburban town with no blacks (excluded by real estate covenants), I met my first blacks at track meets, where they sprinted and I ran the mile. My exposure was increased by having a black friend in my dorm section in college and by doing field work in Brooklyn and Harlem during seminary. I lived and worked in the ghetto during a one-year post-seminary internship in Wilmington, Delaware, and for three years in the Hough section of Cleveland, starting work during the Hough riots, which seemed only to increase the tendency of white suburbanites to avoidance, fear, and escape into art and nature.

Boozed violence breaks out
On Saturday night.
The ghetto's pent-up wrath
Inflicts self-blight.

Shall we steel our nerves
And call the cops in fright?
Or seek to find a way
To set the wrong things right?

---

[87] My poem "Mission"

The artist holds a fragrant flower
Before his painted nose.
He cannot see the blood-stained world
That seethes beyond his toes.

Is nature's green the balm
For all of mankind's woes
Or are black and white the hues
In which compassion grows?[88]

My ministry in inner-city Cleveland revolved around work with youth and community involvement. In conjunction with Southern Christian Leadership Conference's "Operation Breadbasket," we asked a grocery chain to hire and promote more blacks. Our plea was ignored so we organized a boycott. With produce rotting on the shelves, the chain responded to our countervailing power and agreed to our plan. Dr. Martin Luther King, Jr. came up from Atlanta to celebrate our victory, and I got to shake his hand along with other ministers from black churches. When funding ran out for my position, I applied to other churches and to grad school. During those "black power" days, black churches wanted black ministers, and I was too blackened by my experience for white churches to want me. But grad school accepted me, and I went there, in part, to supplement my view from the trenches with more of an overview of our racist society.

Few of my classes in Berkeley dealt extensively with race, but I did join a group ministry called Project Understanding, which assisted six congregations in Livermore and Pleasanton to understand and counteract their white racism. We participated in considerable training in the psychological roots of racism in defensiveness, learning techniques for exposing fear, guilt, and anger and moving on to constructive action. I grew a lot in the process.

I wonder if I dare
Confront the whole of me.
Am I a spreading tree
And am I free to share?
I really learned to care,
To fight, to dance, to be.
I trained my eyes to see
And left my anger there.

---

[88] My poem "Compassion"

The exquisite odor of lotion,
The mystique of a candlelight shower.
The elan of a hike's upward motion.
The release of our unbridled power.
The encradling of caring devotion--
All combined in our group's finest hour.[89]

Over time my concern for civil rights has expanded to include women's rights, men's liberation, and gay rights and issues of class as well as race. I taught a course on Poverty and Society at Butler, in which mostly affluent students were exposed to poor people and their concerns. Joining demonstrations for Justice for Janitors and for immigration rights has linked me with a mainly Hispanic segment.

Seeking peace has also been a major concern for me. When reading Homer in Greek in college, I was struck by how the Greeks, so mature and logical in much of their thinking, had a blind spot when it came to war, not questioning it philosophically but taking it for granted and glorifying it. In Homeric style, I mourn the fate of Lykaon:

Hurl his body on the dark life-gulfing water,
Sacrificed to Xanthos, mighty flowing river.
Hurl this wounded, naked suppliant whose liver
Dread Achilles clove. This son of Altes' daughter--
Now sea-tombed, rain-mourned--
          heart-piercing grief has brought her,
Who will never see him more. A silver sliver
In the pool of Death, his tattered corpse shall shiver
While bloodthirsty fish complete the ruthless slaughter.

The time will come when men will murder hateful war
Nor ever after deign to shed a brother's blood,
To stain the dark life-giving earth with gore no more
Nor torch a pyre and bury heroes bones in mud.
For War himself they shall entomb by Ocean's door
Within a peaceful glade where lovers pluck Spring's bud.[90]

In California, it was the Vietnam War that I protested along with members of a church for which I worked. Like Iraq today, this was not a just war by any means. Going against the notion of sacrifice which bolsters the religion of war, I grieve the human cost:

[89] My poem "Release"
[90] My poem "Lament to Lykaon"

They sent Phil's coffin home today,
Gift-wrapped in a flag of blood-spit-sky.
Shrill trumpets bid his corpse good-bye:
A hero's welcome back they bray:
"Be of good cheer. Feel no dismay.
No finer present could he buy
Than in a noble cause to die.
For you, he gave his life away."

Cry out, O ravaged blood-stained earth!
Give answer, bloody blackened sun!
Against the day that gave thee birth
Cry out, my soul, till day is done:
"A country's pride is scarcely worth
The blood of one lone mother's son."[91]

My academic endeavors aimed to think outside the box by seeking a religion which did not make arrogant, imperialistic, unsubstantiated claims but sought to replace exclusion and exploitation with inclusion and cooperation in a capitalist, racist, imperialist, militarist society. The linguistic analysis I encountered in philosophy in college seemed at first to be a comedown from the grand philosophies of the past and seemed to leave no place for religion in its stress on verifiability for all legitimate statements. But this was actually a gift in realizing that religious language is not designed to convey information akin to science but achieves its power by being odd, indeed extraordinary. Like art, religious language works when it is revelatory and inspiring, which may explain why poetry may convey religious insight better than theology. In my seminary master's thesis, "The Case for a Functional Christology," I suggest that a person asserting "Jesus is Lord" may have less to say about Jesus and more to say about what a person is committed to doing (e.g., following Jesus). Historical and even sociological analysis reveals the shape of the Roman imperialism Jesus opposed and suggests what followers then and now may mean when they ascribe lordship to Jesus rather than Caesar and his men. Form criticism of a book like the Bible identifies the various literary forms, including myths, which are to be neither taken "literally" nor to be disparaged but to be interpreted precisely as myth, looking for their symbolic meaning, pointing beyond themselves, in a spirit of symbolic realism. My PhD thesis, "The Kennedy Myth: American Civil Religion in the Sixties," looks at the stories we tell ourselves about an American president during his campaign, presidency, assassination.

---

[91] My poem "A Christmas Present"

Drawing on the work of my mentor Robert Bellah, this thesis benefits from his elucidation of "civil religion," the religious side of politics, parallel to but separate from the ecclesiastical religion of churches, and applies to it categories from his treatment of religious evolution, coming up with three types of civil religion: archaic, historic, and modern. Archaic civil religion deifies the state and modern exalts the individual while historic aligns with transcendent forces or ideas superior to both society and self. For instance, archaic religion favors holy wars in which men sacrifice themselves for their country, modern uses wars to garner resources valued by selfish consumers, and historic judiciously tries to avoid wars except as a last resort. Facing the prospect of being drafted and sent to Vietnam, many youth stood up for peace in the Sixties opposing their culture on this and other fronts. I did research on the California counterculture of that era defining it in terms of nine values and noting the degree to which they were embodied in three Protestant congregations. The values are: natural playfulness, bodily expressiveness, cosmic awareness, honest openness, familial community, dialogical pluralism, participatory democracy, political involvement, and personal responsibility.[92] They suggest an alternative to our dominant culture. A turning from a consumerism which is wrecking our planet toward a simpler and more communal lifestyle would be more fulfilling.

> In this world of care and pleasure
> Interspersed with work and leisure
> How we use the time assigned us
> Spells the choice of light or blindness.
>
> Choked with goods, yet climbing higher,
> We construct out funeral pyre.
> Callous to an anguished earth,
> We have lost our sense of worth.
>
> Where are roots of joy and kindness
> Which will stem our rush to blindness?
> Where the stream whence blessings flow
> More to heal us than we know?
>
> Could it be that our salvation
> Lies in our humanization?
> Learning how to simply be
> Is the road to ecstasy.

---

[92] See Counterculture on my website pages.uindy.edu/~jwolfe

Seize the time, but let it fritter;
Swill the sweet and drain the bitter.
Life itself in all its color--
Both the bright ones and the duller--
Is a gift that sets us free
To be ourselves expressively.
Having gotten, so we give
And losing fear we learn to live.[93]

Looking back on my life as a whole, it makes a lot of sense, and I am going forward with integrity. It has been a good song, a song of faith. My multi-faceted career has not been a success in conventional terms, despite the prognostication of my high school yearbook, yet it certainly has been interesting and worthwhile despite setbacks. My relation with the institutional church has been checkered at best. Full-time employment eluded me, but for years the ministry I did was recognized as a specialized one. I served on the Church and Society committee of the presbytery in Indianapolis until the committee was dissolved, and I did a report on health care reform (it was ignored). Then presbytery decided not to recognize my specialized ministry, and I responded by writing a Liturgy of Disvalidation to mourn my loss of status, retired as a Presbyterian minister at age 60, and wrote a poem affirming my continuing ministry:

If once a priest, then always a priest
It's *character indelibilis*
A gift of grace, a quest for peace,
Compassion for the very least.
Chief jester at the marriage feast.
Pursuer of the golden fleece.
Till love fills all and wars shall cease,
I'll go for God and quell the beast.

There is a juncture where worlds meet,
A time and place where love finds berth,
When scores are settled, joy complete,
Where beards o'erflow with oil of mirth.
'Tis then as one do two hearts beat.
'Tis there descendeth heaven to earth.[93]

---

[93] My poem "Simplicity"
[93] My poem "Priest"

When I turned 65, I retired as a computer programmer, was diagnosed with mild prostate cancer, and worried about running out of energy as I aged. I responded by having radioactive seeds implanted and by finally being initiated into the ManKind Project, which enabled me to plumb and share feelings and aspirations in a supportive atmosphere of non-judgmental unconditional love.

> Of knowing self, I had despaired,
> My shadow trailing long and wide,
> Dark feelings buried deep inside;
> Unlocking no one yet had dared.
> Would that my very soul were bared,
> Released from fear, defensive pride.
> My brothers bid: "With me confide
> Your joys and sorrows freely shared."
>
> I revel in the forest's shade:
> I summon spirits as I sing
> And dance with wildness in the glade.
> A key retrieves the golden ring:
> I venture forward unafraid
> To pass the blessings of my king.[94]

I emerged from initiation with the affirmation "As a man among men, I am alive with energy" and a clearer sense of mission. My mission is: "I create a world of unbounded love and thought where bodies and souls are nourished and nurtured by doing the political and personal work needed in tune with the divine within and beyond."

I also embraced my Elderhood with its decline and its opportunity to share my wisdom.

> I shall not longer see the sun.
> My days are numbered, one by one.
> My beard is gray; my hair is dun.
> Old-age diseasing has begun.
>
> As Elder, I will teach my son,
> Share age-old wisdom I have won.
> I'll dance my days till days are done
> And take my ease: it will be fun.[95]

---

[94] My poem "Initiation"
[95] My poem "Turning Sixty-five"

My spirituality was further deepened and expanded by participation in Mankind Project rituals. Meetings and retreats often begin with calling in energy from different directions, associated with Jungian archetypes of lover, warrior, king, and magician. Sweat lodges are a time for purification and renewal. These rituals drawn from native American religions gave me a chance to exercise my primitive side and helped me to resolve my issue of how to relate to wicca, about which I was stuck for several years in writing up my theology here.

I had long been aware of the need to re-enchant a disenchanted world and was taken with Norman O. Brown's paean to magic and madness:

> Psychoanalysis began as a further advance of civilized (scientific) objectivity: to expose remnants of primitive participation, to eliminate them; studying the world of dreams, of primitive magic, of madness, but not participating in dreams or magic or madness. But the outcome of psychoanalysis is that magic and madness are everywhere, and dreams is what we are made of. The goal cannot be the elimination of magical thinking or madness; the goal can only be conscious magic or conscious madness; conscious mastery of these fires. And dreaming while awake.[96]

My problem was that, as a scientific person, I did not believe that magic causes events, such as making crops grow. So I dropped that but kept the fuzzier notion of concentrating spiritual energy. There is good and bad in every religion, and my approach is to combine the best of each. My singing of faith is not a monotone but has rich harmonies. I started with Christianity and added others as antidotes and supplements: Jewish Sabbath services in college, Zen in California, Taoism after a Warrior Monk retreat, Islam since 9/11, wicca when unstuck, discussion with local and national humanists.

My motto is: Why have one religion when you can have several? From my Jewish faith, I derive a commitment to justice and to "tikkun olam" (repairing the world). From my Christian faith, I add love and forgiveness. From my Buddhist faith, I generate compassion and paying attention. From my Taoist faith, I practice inner peace and flexible strength. From my Muslim faith, I draw kindness and concern for the poor. From my Wiccan faith, I recover closeness to nature and protection for Mother Earth. From my Humanist faith, I venture into freedom of thought and building a human community. I celebrate all this religious diversity within myself and among us.

---

[96] Norman O. Brown, "Love's Body," p. 254.

APPENDIX: FOUR HYMNS

A Christmas Carol

Far from the crystal palace,
Far from plenty's horn,
Far from alb and chalice,
God's man-child was born.

Out of rooms at the hostel,
Out of a home to nest,
Out of all but a Gospel,
Jesus had no rest.

Scorned by friends and neighbors,
Scorned by the Pharisees,
Scorned by those helped by his labors,
Jesus healed disease.

Stripped of his simple clothing,
Stripped of life and breath,
Stripped of all but loathing,
Jesus met his death.

Closed in a shroud and spices,
Closed in a rich man's grave,
Closed in Satan's vices,
Christ broke free to save.

Clad in splendid raiment,
Robed in rays of light,
Sent as God's first payment,
Christ dispels the night.

Praised by angels glorious,
Christ by all adored,
Over powers victorious,
Jesus rules as Lord.

Hope for the downtrodden,
Good news for the poor,
Rest for the heavy-laden,
Jesus is the door.

King of kings forever,
Bread of life for all,
Priest whom none can sever,
Born in a manger stall.

Jesus

Behold the baby in the straw.
Among the sheep and goats he lies.
The manger smells are rank and raw,
And 'round the piles of dung are flies.
Yet this poor babe is served by kings,
Who tailed a star to David's town.
They laud him with exotic things:
Embalming spice, perfume, and crown.

Behold the glutton and the drunk,
A friend of publicans and whores.
Perceive the depths to which he's sunk:
He touches lepers full of sores.
Yet in his love are dregs made whole;
His healing leaves his garment's hem.
The worker finds rest for his soul;
The poor have good news preached to them.

"Behold the man," snide Pilate said.
"Is this your king, you Jewish swine?
With crown of thorns we'll deck his head;
Upon a cross he'll look divine."
Yet that same rood so full of pain
Became the place he held his court,
Forgiving those who nailed in vain
And giving thieves a last resort.

Behold the servant of the Lord,
A man of sorrows and of grief,
Whose lifework jangles with discord,
Whose message is beyond belief.
Yet by his stripes have we been healed.
We lay our burdens at his feet.
The Lord's strong arm has been revealed:
We dance to this new piper's beat.

A Pharisee and a Publican

A Pharisee and a publican
Went into the temple to pray.
The one thanked God,
    the other's tears ran,
And then they went their way.

The Pharisee gave his thanks to God
That he's not like other folks.
In righteousness his feet have trod;
He tithes, he fasts, no jokes.

The publican beat upon his breast,
And his clothes he began to rend:
"My sins have given me no rest.
Forgive me, O God, my friend."

A Pharisee and a publican
Went into the temple to pray.
The one met God,
    the other praised man,
And then they went their way.

In meeting God we are justified
When we go to the church
    to praise
The One who batters down
    our pride
And humble folks with raise.

A Song of Love

I sing a song of the love of God
Who made a world for me
With trees and birds
    and lakes and sod
And my own fair body.

I sing a song of the love of Christ
Whose life has set me free:
I'm split and drained and drawn
    and spliced
To every creature I see.

I sing a song of the love of Sprite,
Who dances like a bee.
She stings and strokes and frees
    from fright
And leads me on a spree.

I sing a song of the love of Man,
Who brings me ecstasy.
I'll wrap my arms round him
    if I can
And cherish his company.

I sing a song of the joy of love,
In God and man burst free.
From earth below to heaven above
I'll sing eternally.

Different is Good (Children's Sermon)

There is a children's song called "Reuben and Rachel." Maybe you have sung it. It goes like this. First the boys sing:
    Reuben, Reuben, I've been thinking what a fine world this would be
    If the girls were all transported far beyond the northern sea.
Then the girls sing:
    Rachel, Rachel, I've been thinking what a fine world this would be
    If the boys were all transported far beyond the northern sea.
Of course, this song is all in fun, but it is actually a scary prospect to think of half the human race being removed far away. Although it is fine for boys and girls to borrow traits that supposedly belong to the other, it is also good that boys and girls are different. And, as the French say, "Vive la difference!"--let the difference thrive.

There are groups of people who want everyone to be the same and hate people who are different. One such group is the Ku Klux Klan. They hate blacks, gays, Jews, Catholics, and anyone else who is different from them. But they have no monopoly on hate.

As you well know, children can be very cruel--and so can teenagers. It is very easy to make fun of kids who are different. Some kids wear clothes that set them apart; some are fat; some have certain skills and lack others.I know. I liked to read books as a child and won the book-reading contest in first grade, and I did very well in school. But I stunk at the major sports: football, basketball, and baseball. I was labeled as a "bookworm" and a "brain," and maybe a bit of a "sissy." I got no respect. But then a funny thing happened. I discovered that running, which I had done all my life because I was always running late, was a sport, and I excelled as a track star. So then I became somewhat popular. I ran the mile in 4 minutes, 43 seconds during my sophomore year in high school and served as captain of the cross-country team my senior year, And a fellow brain and I were even honored in the high school yearbook as seniors "most likely to succeed." Not ong ago, I succeeded in earning Presidential Sports Awards in bicycling, tennis, and golf. However, I am almost glad I spent some time on the other side of the tracks because it gives me more sympathy for the underdog.

I like to pal around with people who are weird and different, and I am not afraid to be different myself. One silly way in which I am different is that I like the smell of skunk if it is not too powerful. Now the poor skunk has few friends. He is hard to get close to, and he is a stinker! But then so am I. Like I said, there are lots of sports I stink at--though I don't play them now. Like everyone else, I have special strengths and weaknesses, and I believe that God, my Creator, has a hand in that. My wife gave me a skunk for my mascot. I brought him along. As you can see, he comes with a message: "God made me special."

I am special. And you are special. We are all special. God made us that way. God made the world with a great variety of plants and animals and a great variety among human beings. Our life is enriched by this, for "variety is the spice of life." I encourage people to develop their specialties, and I respect ways in which they are different from me--and I would suggest that you do likewise. When you run across someone different from most, reach out and befriend him or her. And when someone fails to appreciate your specialties, do not sulk or withdraw. Remember that we have a secret weapon:

it is love. Love is stronger than hate. There is a group of people who ride bicycles with me when I ride in the Mad Madison to raise money for multiple sclerosis. They are called Hate Busters, and they wear shirts--like the ghostbuster ones--with a big line crossing out the word HATE. Some in this group themselves have multiple sclerosis, so they know what it is like to be rejected because they are crippled. But they do not take abuse lying down. They are up and riding, some slower than the rest, some in great pain. But they are out there flaunting their differences and proclaiming a message of love over hate. There is a short poem by Edwin Markham that puts it so well. Let me explain a few big words before I recite it. A "heretic"is a person who has beliefs different from most, and a "rebel" is someone who refuses to act like everyone else; "flouting" is teasing and rejecting.

> He drew a circle that shut me out,
> Heretic, rebel, a thing to flout.
> But love and I had the wit to win:
> We drew a circle that took him in.

As Christians, we believe in the power of love, and we try to draw the biggest circles we can--taking all sorts of people in. Jesus came that we all might be one. "Christ is our peace, who breaks down the dividing walls of hostility between us," said St. Paul. He saw that people made a big deal of differences, but he said they did not matter: "In Christ, there is neither Jew nor Greek, male nor female, slave nor free, but all are one in Christ Jesus."

Paul said that the church is the body of Christ, and a body only works if it has different parts. If a body were all eyes, how could it hear? If it were all ears, how could it see? And how stupid it is for the hand to say to the foot, "I don't need you." I know this from tennis. There is very little the hand holding my racket can do if my feet are not in position. No, we all need each other in the church, and each of us has special gifts which we need to exercise in the work of the church, respecting those whose gifts and work are different from our own. The church and the world are full of differences. We celebrate that. As the Arby's slogan puts it: "Different is good."

INDEX

Index (2)

Index (3)

Index (4)

Index to Scriptures

Scripture index (2)

Index to My Poems

Bibliography

Bellah, Robert N.
1970 <u>Beyond Belief</u>. New York: Harper & Row.

Black Elk (as recorded by John G. Niehardt).
1932 <u>Black Elks Speaks</u>. Lincoln: University of Nebraska Press.

Brown, Norman O.
1966 <u>Love's Body</u>. New York: Random House.

Campbell, Joseph (with Bill Moyers).
1988 <u>The Power of Myth</u>. New York: Doubleday.

Cox, Harvey.
1969 <u>Feast of Fools</u>. Cambridge, MA: Harvard Univ. Press.

Durkheim, Emile.
1915 <u>Elementary Forms of the Religious Life</u>. New York: Free Press.

Frazier, James.
1922 <u>The Golden Bough</u>. Toronto: MacMillan.

Gibran, Kahlil.
1951 <u>The Prophet</u>. New York: Knopf.

Jeffers, Susan.
1991 <u>Brother Eagle, Sister Sky</u>. New York: Dial Books.

Satir, Virginia.
1967 <u>Conjoint Family Therapy</u>. Palo Alto: Science & Behavior Books.

<u>Tao te Ching</u>. Tr. Gia-Fu Feng and Jane English. New York: Random House.

Tillich, Paul.
1951 <u>Systematic Theology</u>. Chicago: Univ. of Chicago Press

Wilber, Ken
2001 <u>No Boundary</u>. Boston: Shambhala Publications.

<u>A Winter Solstice Singing Ritual</u>. Sebastopol, CA: Emerald Earth Pub.

Preface to "The Gist of the Bible"

Some people try to read the whole Bible from cover to cover in a year. With the best of intentions, many shipwreck on the first genealogy in Genesis or get bogged down in the Holiness Code in Leviticus. Even those who succeed, cover so much material that they often lose sight of the forest for the trees. The approach in "The Gist of the Bible" is quite different. I have selected what I consider the 104 best chapters in the Bible so a person could read two chapters a week and get a sense of the gist of the whole book and its major themes. There is an attempt to achieve both depth and breadth. The whole Gospel of Mark, the earliest gospel which is the basis for much in Matthew and Luke, is read along with several distinctive chapters from the other gospels. At least one chapter from most of the major books in the Bible is also included.

Readings 1-26 feature the Hebrew Bible (Old Testament) and are recommended to be read from June through November; readings 27-52 focus mainly on the New Testament and are to be read in December through May (Advent through Pentecost). One may wish to move some readings dealing with the teachings of Jesus until after Pentecost in a year when Easter comes early so that accounts of the death and resurrection of Jesus fall in holy week.

These readings can be used in personal study or in group classes or in corporate worship. I have prepared 16-line commentaries on each pair of chapters, which can be studied alone or discussed in class or read in church as a "Minute for the Word." The commentaries seek to bring out the meaning of the chapters, their historical context, their literary form, and their place in the section or strand of which they are a part--bringing what most scholars and ministers know to folks in the pew. The major sections of the Hebrew Bible are the Law (Genesis-Deuteronomy), the Prophets (Joshua-Malachi), and the Writings (Job-Song of Solomon--which come last in the Hebrew Bible but separate historical from prophetic Prophets in the Old Testament). The major sections in the New Testament are the Gospels-plus-Acts (Luke-Acts is one work), the letters of Paul from longest to shortest, the Pastoral Epistles, Hebrews, James, the Catholic Epistles, and Revelation. The chief strands in the Law and beyond are "J" (a southern Davidic writer who calls God "Jehovah"), "E" (a northern source which calls God "Elohim"), "D" (Deuteronomist associated with Josiah's reforms), and "P" (post-exilic priestly one).

A Year's Bible Readings

1.	Creation:	Genesis 1	Psalm 8
2.	Man and Woman:	Genesis 2	Song of Solomon 2
3.	Fall/Redemption:	Genesis 3	Romans 5
4.	Abraham's Faith:	Genesis 12	Hebrews 11
5.	Deliverance:	Exodus 3	Exodus 15
6.	Commandments:	Exodus 20	Deuteronomy 5
7.	Laws:	Deuteronomy 6	Leviticus 19
8.	Conquest:	Joshua 6	Judges 5
9.	Faith/Disloyalty:	Joshua 24	Exodus 32
10.	Being Called:	I Samuel 3	Isaiah 6
11.	Against Monarchy:	I Samuel 8	I Samuel 10
12.	King David:	II Samuel 5	II Samuel 12
13.	Temple:	II Samuel 7	I Kings 8
14.	God versus Baal:	I Kings 18	Hosea 2
15.	God's Judgment	Isaiah 1	Amos 5
16.	God's Holiness	Micah 6	Hosea 11
17.	Exile	Jeremiah 20	II Kings 25
18.	Lament	Lamentations 1	Psalm 137
19.	Despair and Hope	Job 19	Psalm 22
20.	Lord as Shepherd	Psalm 23	John 10
21.	Forgiveness	Psalm 51	Luke 15
22.	Time and Eternity	Psalm 90	Ecclesiastes 3
23.	Praise	Psalm 100	Psalm 150
24.	Wisdom and Help	Proverbs 3	James 2
25.	Vision	Ezekiel 37	Jeremiah 31
26.	Restoration	Ezra 6	Nehemiah 9
27.	Promise	Isaiah 40	Isaiah 9
28.	God's Triumph	Daniel 7	Revelation 19
29.	Hope and Love	I John 3	I Corinthians 13
30.	Incarnation	Luke 1	John 1
31.	Birth of Jesus	Luke 2	Matthew 2
32.	Mission	Mark 1	Luke 4
33.	Abandon	Mark 2	Luke 7
34.	Commissioning	Mark 3	Luke 10
35.	Kingdom of God	Mark 4	Matthew 5
36.	Rebirth	Mark 5	John 3
37.	Bread of Heaven	Mark 6	John 6
38.	Freedom and Purity	Mark 7	Galatians 5
39.	Suffering	Mark 8	Hebrews 2
40.	Transfiguration	Mark 9	II Corinthians 5
41.	Servanthood	Mark 10	John 13
42.	Authority	Mark 11	Romans 13
43.	Cornerstone	Mark 12	I Peter 2
44.	Final Judgment	Mark 13	Matthew 25
45.	Last Supper	Mark 14	I Corinthians 11
46.	Crucifixion	Mark 15	Isaiah 53
47.	Resurrection	Mark 16	I Corinthians 15
48.	Ascension	Luke 24	Acts 1
49.	Christ's Spirit	Acts 2	Philippians 2
50.	Church Universal	Acts 7	Acts 10
51.	Body and Vine	I Corinthians 12	John 15
52.	Consummation	Revelations 21	Romans 8

1.   Creation: Genesis 1   Psalm 8

A year with the Bible. Where should we begin? At the beginning.   "In the beginning God" is how the Bible begins. The first creation story (in Genesis 1) is not the first passage written. It is part of the prologue to a saga that begins with Abraham and culminates in the Exodus. It comes from a strand in the Hebrew Bible that scholars call "P," the priestly source. It reflects the rather late belief that God is not only God of the Jews but also creator of all. This scripture is a responsive reading. It does not try to describe the world's evolution scientifically but to celebrate receiving the world from God's hands. God stills mighty winds[1] as he brings order out of chaos. God forms sun, moon, stars, plants, birds, fish, animals and humankind, made in God's image to tend God's creation.[2] Psalm 8 is even more clearly a song for worship, singing of God's glory and man's derived glory, who is little less than divine. In the convention in Hebrew poetry which expresses the same idea twice, it asks what is man that God thinks of him and the son of man that God cares for him[3].

2.   Man and Woman: Genesis 2   Song of Solomon 2

The prologue to Genesis continues with a second creation story, which is quite different from the first: not a lofty liturgy but a folk tale. Here God does not speak the world into being but (within a world already presumed present) takes dirt and blows breath into it so that man--whose name "Adam" means "earthling"--becomes a living creature[4].   When fellow animals did not provide adequate companionship, God formed woman from man. Man greets woman with poetry and the two became one flesh, naked and unashamed. Love poetry is also featured in the Song of Solomon. In the second chapter, a maiden portrays her beloved as a bounding young stag who beckons her to arise and bloom with delight like springtime flowers. The passage is unabashedly rife with sexual overtones. The Song comes from a segment of the Hebrew Bible called the Writings, considered supplementary to the Law and the Prophets. Genesis 2 comes from a strand scholars call "J" because God is called Jehovah, God's own name (though translations substitute the generic LORD)[5].

---

[1] Hebrew: *ruah elohim* was traditionally but questionably translated "Spirit of God."
[2] Hebrew *tselem*: Near Eastern kings would equip their ambassadors with their image.
[3] *Ben adam*, "son of man," is not a title but a synonym for "man." ("mortal man" NEB)
[4] *Nephesh hayah* is the same word used for animals; living "being" or "soul" is poor.
[5] In reading scripture, the pious Jew says *adonai* "Lord" whenever he sees *YHWH*.

3.   Fall/Redemption: Genesis 3   Romans 5

The folk tale recounting God's creation of man in Genesis 2 proceeds into Genesis 3 in an account traditionally known as the "fall of man." This chapter contains primitive explanations of why man is mortal, why men must toil, why childbirth is painful, why snakes are legless but reflects profoundly on the human condition. As myth, a timeless story, it portrays our coming into firsthand knowledge[6] of good and evil. For both early humans and each child, this dawn of moral consciousness is a descent and an ascent. It is experienced as a loss of innocence, shame in nakedness, and expulsion from paradise but also as maturity and freedom. We humans are perennially tempted to forget that we are earthlings, created by God and subject to divine guidance, as we aspire to be like God, who alone knows fully what is right and wrong. In our self-righteousness, we distance ourselves from God. But God has bridged the gap, St. Paul tells us in Romans 5, in Jesus Christ, who represents a new redeemed humanity reconciled to God by God's grace and receiving righteousness as a gift in faith.

4.   Abraham's Faith: Genesis 12   Hebrews 11 [11:1-12:2]

After the prologue in Genesis 1-11, the saga of the Hebrews begins with the patriarch Abram in Genesis 12. Abraham[7] is a man of faith because he trusts in God and in God's promises. At God's command, he leaves his homeland and journeys to an unknown land that God has promised him: moving from Mesopotamia to Shechem, Bethel, Egypt, and Hebron. Abraham believes God's promise that he will be father of a mighty nation through whom all nations will be blessed even though he has sent away his concubine Hagar and son Ishmael (the father of the Arabs), even though his wife Sarah was childless and beyond childbearing age, even though he was ready to sacrifice his son Isaac at God's command until God relented. Hebrews 11 sees the faith of Abraham as pivotal among a great cloud of witnesses seeing faith as assurance of things hoped for, conviction of things not seen. Faith discerns the creativity of God in bringing new things into being and perseveres in seeking a heavenly city despite hardships. Hebrews portrays a tempted, suffering Jesus as pioneer and perfecter of faith

---

6 In Hebrew, *yadah* is not abstract but experiential and even carnal knowledge.

7 God renames *Abram*, "elevated father," *Abraham*, "father of multitudes" in Gen. 17:5.

5.   Deliverance: Exodus 3   Exodus 15

The exodus from Egypt is the central event in the Hebrew Bible. In Exodus 3, God attracts the attention of Moses through a burning bush, tells him God feels the sufferings of the Hebrews as slaves in Egypt, and sends Moses to go down to Egypt to lead his people out[8]. Moses tells God that saying that the God of their fathers is backing him would not be enough; he needs to know God's own name if he is to convince the people to take the risk of following him. God's name is full of reassurance. It is "I will make to be what I will make to be."[9] God reveals himself as lord of history who will intimidate pharaoh with wonders and lead his people from oppression in Egypt to freedom in a bountiful land. Exodus 15 celebrates the Egyptian horsemen being bogged down in the sea of reeds[10] while the Hebrews escaped. Exodus 15, which contains the oldest and most primitive view of God in the Bible, "Jehovah is a man of war", comes from "J" while Exodus 3 comes from "E" a strand whose author usually calls God "Elohim" and calls the holy mountain Horeb rather than Sinai.

6.   Commandments: Exodus 20   Deuteronomy 5

The God who delivered the Hebrews from bondage in Egypt follows up by giving Moses the Ten Commandments on Mount Sinai on the trek from Egypt to Canaan. Other nations have their gods, but the Hebrews are forbidden to make images of them or to worship them. They are forbidden to use God's name in magic or for a smokescreen so as to appear pious[11]. To commemorate God's rest after creation, they are to keep the sabbath holy and free of work for themselves, servants, animals, strangers[12]. They are told to honor their parents. The Hebrews are generally free but are prohibited from taking the life of another, except in war or capital punishment, and from taking, directly or through the courts, what does not belong to them, whether wives, animals, or goods (stealing, adultery, coveting). They are also enjoined from bearing false witness in legal disputes. The commandments in Exodus 20 (from "J") are also repeated by the Deuteronomist (source "D") in Deuteronomy 5, which reminds listeners that they lacked sabbath as a day off when slaves in Egypt.

---

[8] *Ex-odos* in Greek means "the way out;" *Genesis* means "beginning" or "origin."

[9] The sacred name *YHWH*, printed without vowels, could be in the causative tense.

[10] *Yom suf* means "sea of reeds." Reeds can be reddish, but "Red Sea" is mistranslation.

[11] Bandying God's name as if it meant nothing real is taking it *la-shua*, "in vain."

[12] *Shabbat* runs from Friday sundown to Saturday sundown; Christians meet on Sunday.

7.   Laws: Deuteronomy 6   Leviticus 19

Deuteronomy 6 contains the Shema, still prominent in the Jewish sabbath service, which affirms the late belief in the oneness of God and commands us to love God with all our heart, spirit, and might.[13] Reminders of law are to be posted on forehead, hand, and doorposts. One should talk of law at home and on the street, at dawn and night; it should be taught to children as a sequel to the saga of the Exodus. Deuteronomy was discovered in a cleansing of the Jerusalem Temple in 821 B.C. under King Josiah and was included to conclude the Torah. Leviticus contains a holiness code from the priestly source ("P").[14] Many of the Ten Commandments are reiterated and amplified here so that swearing by God's name in order to hoodwink is prohibited as is stealing by withholding wages or using false weights. Gleanings from fields and vineyards are reserved for strangers and the poor. There is concern for violation of ritual purity as in eating sacrificed meat three days later.[15] Rather than hatred, vengeance, and grudges, you should reason with your neighbor and love neighbor as yourself.

8.   Conquest: Joshua 6   Judges 5

Joshua begins the historical and prophetic books called the Prophets. Joshua took over the leadership of the Hebrews after the death of Moses and led the conquest. Joshua 6 tells the conquest of Jericho. Since Jericho had no walls at the time, the tale of Jericho's capture has been embellished with trumpets sounding and walls falling over. The rules of holy war required the destruction of everyone and every thing in the conquered city, except precious metals devoted to God. Rahab the prostitute, however, is spared along with her relatives because she had hidden the Hebrew spies. Military leaders, such as Samson, Gideon, and Deborah the Prophetess, were called judges.[16] Most history comes from "D," but the Song of Deborah in Judges 5, the oldest passage in the Bible, comes through "J" (note Mt. Sinai). Deborah celebrates the defeat of the Canaanites in the Jezreel Valley near Megiddo with help from the flooding river Kishon and the killing of their escaped leader Sisera by Jael the Kenite. The degree of participation by eight Hebrew tribes and two sub-tribes is noted.

---

[13] These facets overlap; *lev* is heart/mind; *nephesh* is spirit/breath; *maoth* is forceful.
[14] *Deutero-nomos* means "seconded law" in Greek; *Levitikos* suggests levitical priests.
[15] *Pigul* is "uncleanness," overstated when translated as "abomination."
[16] Though *shophetim* had some judicial functions, they were more generals than judges.

9.   Dedication/Idolatry: Joshua 24   Exodus 32

The invasion of the plains of Canaan by the hill-dwelling Hebrew tribes was a piecemeal process. They may not all have been blood relatives or all taken part in the Exodus, but they bonded themselves as the Israelites, descendants of the sons of Jacob[17], and adopted the story of the exodus from Egypt as their story. In Joshua 24, after hearing Joshua recount God's giving Abraham offspring, saving Moses, and giving them power to conquer, the twelve tribes of Israel covenanted together in a military and political alliance in Shechem. The covenant required serving Jehovah exclusively and getting rid of foreign gods, such as Canaanite gods, Egyptian gods, or gods whom Abram's kin worshipped in Mesopotamia[18]. The Israelites were told that their jealous God would consume them if they fell into idolatry. Earlier many died by the swords of the sons of Levi or by plague after they had made and worshiped a golden calf when Moses was on Sinai, as recorded in Exodus 32. Now Joshua challenged Israel to choose whom they would serve; he and they chose to serve the LORD.

10.   Being Called: I Samuel 3   Isaiah 6

Prophets hear voices and see visions and then they speak forth what God has revealed. The historical books of Samuel and Kings come from "D" and are paralleled in the royal chronicles. In I Samuel 3, young Samuel hears a voice calling him, which he eventually identifies as God's, and is given the onerous task of pronouncing the doom of his mentor's house. In Isaiah 6, as recorded by Isaiah's disciples, we read of the vision of God which Isaiah of Jerusalem had during the troubles following the death of King Uzziah in 742 BC. Isaiah envisions God enthroned in the Temple in Jerusalem attended by winged serpents[19] who chant that God is holy and the earth heavy with God's presence.[20] Face to face with this holy King, Isaiah feels unclean but his guilt is purged by a burning coal from the altar. When God asks whom to send, Isaiah answers, "Here I am! Send me." God tells Isaiah to keep preaching his message even though it will not be understood until cities are laid waste and people carted away but promises that a stump will remain as a source of holy seed.

---

[17] *Isra-el*, "he who wrestles with God," was an epithet that Jacob won, Genesis 32:28.

[18] *Meso-potamia* is Greek for the land "between the rivers" Tigris and Euphrates.

[19] *Seraphim* in Hebrew, akin to Sanskrit, *sarpa*, serpent: see Num. 21:8, II Kings 18:4.

[20] The roots for *qadosh*, holy, is "clean" and for *kevadh*, glory, is "heavy."

11.　Against Monarchy:　I Samuel 8　I Samuel 10

When much of Canaan had been taken over by the Israelites through a combination of invasion, migration, and internal revolt, the elders asked Samuel to give them a king so they could be like other nations. Samuel warned them that they would become slaves again if they had a king. He would impress their sons and daughters into his service as soldiers, farmers, and cooks. A professional standing army and taxes to support and equip it would replace emergency citizen footsoldiers. Land rights, protected through the law against coveting and through periodic land redistribution, would give way to royal confiscation of land, servants, and livestock. Social equality before God would be replaced by social stratification under the king. When the people insisted that they needed a king to fight battles, God told Samuel to go along even though they rejected God as king. Saul was selected by lot and anointed by Samuel to be messiah.[21] God gave King Saul a new heart and the spirit of God came upon him, leading to ecstatic speech; later Saul lost his spirit and authority.

12.　King David:　II Samuel 5 II Samuel 12

After Saul went bad, the elders of Israel anointed David as messiah. As king, David continued his military successes and expanded Israelite holdings. He captured the Jebusite sity of Jerusalem by going up its water system and made it his capital. He built a palace there and acquired concubines, wives, and children. David took the crown of the king of Rabbah and impressed the inhabitants of this and other defeated Canaanite cities into his labor crews. David was much admired, but he also sinned and brought a curse upon his house. David coveted Bathsheba whom he saw bathing on the rooftop; he committed adultery with her; he tried to get her husband, Uriah the Hittite, to lie with her to cloud his paternity, and then he sent Uriah into the forefront of battle where he was killed. Nathan the prophet confronted the king. Nathan got David to pass judgment on himself. The king in Israel is not above the law, which applies to foreign mercenaries as well as Israelites. The first child of Bathsheba died, but her next child Solomon succeeded David after a family struggle.

---

[21] The *meshiakh* is a man anointed by God to be king; the Greek equivalent is *christos*.

13.   Temple: II Samuel 7 I Kings 8

King David offered to build God a house, but God promised instead to build David's house, to make him a great name, to be like a father to him, to chasten him but never to remove his steadfast love from him. God revealed his name to Moses and made a name for himself by redeeming Israel from Egypt, and now God's name is being magnified as his presence and influence are felt in a growing Davidic kingdom. King Solomon built a Temple in Jerusalem for God's name. He had the ark of the covenant, containing two tablets of stone engraved with the Ten Commandments put into the Holy of Holies, supported by two cherubim, statues with lion body and head of a man plus wings that hid the ark. Solomon prayed that God would keep his covenant[22] with the sons of David if they continued to be faithful to him, that God would listen to prayers directed to him in or toward the Temple by Israelites or by foreigners, and that God would forgive and restore those who acknowledged their sins and repented after suffering defeat, drought, famine, sickness, or exile. Then they feasted.

14.   God versus Baal: I Kings 18   Hosea 2

The Israelites had long combined their worship of Jehovah with fertility rites absorbed from the Canaanites, who were far more experienced in raising successful crops. Sacrificing to the husband, or *baal*, of each plot of ground was believed to make it fruitful, and sex with a cult prostitute was thought to fertilize the crops. After Solomon's death, the kingdom split into Israel and Judah. Kings often took foreign wives to seal alliances and allowed wives to keep their own gods. King Ahab of Israel allowed his Phoenician wife Jezebel to install Baal-Melkart and his consort the goddess Asherah in the temple in his capital city Samaria while suppressing prophets of Jehovah. According to legend, Elijah held a contest with the priests of Baal who proved powerless while Elijah's invocation of Jehovah was followed by fire upon the altar and rain ending drought. Hosea took a cult prostitute for a wife buying her from the cult. This parallels Jehovah restoring Israel after she played the harlot with Baal, returning to first husband, source of grain, wine, and oil.

---

22 *B'rith*, covenant, is an agreement; *hesed* is covenanted, steadfast love.

15. God's Judgment   Isaiah 1   Amos 5

Although Amos spoke to Israel in the ninth century B.C. and Isaiah spoke to Judah in the eighth, their messages are very similar. Both condemned injustice, disparaged religiosity, foresaw destruction, appealed for repentance, and foretold God's mercy upon a remnant. God is judging his people for rebelling by taking bribes, cheating the poor, and neglecting widows and orphans. God is not hoodwinked by sacrifices and feasts and the noise of solemn assemblies; tramping his courts does not make up for trampling the poor. With Assyria and Babylon threatening from without and corruption festering within, the prophets foresaw the desolation of Israel and Judah, wailing in cities and fields, fine houses emptied, and the population decimated. Judgment can be averted if the people correct oppression and let justice roll down like waters; if not, judgment will purge the people of their sins and wash them white as snow upon the day of the Lord. After judgment, God's gracious restoration is envisioned marked by the reign of justice under faithful leaders as of old.

16. God's Holiness   Micah 6   Hosea 11

Like their respective contemporaries Amos and Isaiah, Hosea in the north and Micah in the south were prophets of doom and hope. Both appear in the section of twelve "minor," i.e., shorter prophetic books, books with textual uncertaincies, disparities in chapter breaks, and interpolations of anonymous prophetic sayings[23]. Both see rebellion against God, manifest in worshiping idols and in deceitful weights, resulting in deprivation and desolation. Both remind their listeners of God's rescuing Israel from Egypt. Hosea portrays God as loving Israel like a son and feeling warm compassion for him. The holiness of God prevents destroying Israel in anger, as man might do, and impels reaching out to him and calling him back home from exile. Holiness[24] is not the wrath of the pure recoiling from the impure but disciplining and bending down in love to feed the wayward child. Likewise the holiness that God requires of man does not involve animal or human sacrifice (as practiced by Judah's King Manasseh[25]) but walking with God in justice and mercy and faith.

---

23 Hosea 11:12 begins chapter 12 in Hebrew; only Micah 1-3 is assuredly from Micah.

24 The original root of *qadosh*, holy, is "clean," but the meaning has been expanded now.

25 Since Manasseh sacrificed his son (II Kings 21:6), a prophet of that era speaks here.

17.   Exile   Jeremiah 20   II Kings 25

Court prophets were hired by the king to tell him what he wanted to hear. They advised alliance with Egypt and rebellion against Babylon and promised peace. In the short term, they led a pleasant life. Not so Jeremiah. In secret meetings with King Zedekiah and in his public proclamations, recorded by his scribe Baruch, Jeremiah counseled cooperation with Babylon and foresaw destruction, plunder, and captivity as the price of non-cooperation. One time Jeremiah was put in a well to die but was subsequently rescued. This time the chief priest of the Temple beat him and put him in the stocks, where he became a laughingstock. Jeremiah was born to be a prophet but rued the day he was born. He tried to avoid prophesying but could not contain the fire within. What Jeremiah foretold came to pass, as recorded in the conclusion of the deuternomic history in II Kings 25. Nebuchadnezzar king of Babylon beseiged and captured Jerusalem in 586 B.C. Temple and palace were looted and burned. Priests and royal sons were slain. The cream of Judah was carried off to exile.

18.   Lament   Lamentations 1   Psalm 137

In exile, Judah became a laughingstock among the nations. Her foes gloated at her downfall. Babylonian captors taunted the Judeans to sing a song of Zion, but the only sound they can muster is weeping with none to comfort them as they pined for Jerusalem. In lament Jerusalem is portrayed as a lonely widow who has become filthy because of her sins, rightly punished for rebellion against Jehovah. Those who pass by are indifferent to her unparalleled sorrow, and the lovers with which she defiled herself do not keep their promises. Her temple has been desecrated by plundering foreigners[26], and few attend her feasts now that her maidens and young men have been dragged into captivity. Those who are left are desperate for bread. Jerusalem, once a princess among cities, has become a vassal. She remembers what she has lost, and the captive Judeans vow never to forget her. They pray that God will remember those who destroyed Jerusalem and make them pay for their sins as Judah has done. In a spirit of revenge, they imagine their captors' babies dashed to death.

---

26 *Goyim*, foreign "nations" or Gentiles, were allowed only in the Temple's outer courts.

19. Despair and Hope   Job 19   Psalm 22

Job is a folk tale. It begins the Writings section of the Hebrew Bible. It is a piece of wisdom literature, dealing with general themes, not with Jewish history; its main character Job is an Edomite,not a Jew. The prologue introduces a new figure, the Adversary[27], who bets that Job is righteous only because it pays to be so. To test this notion, God allows Job to be visited with calamity: loss of livestock and servants, deaths of all his children, sores on his body. Comforters tell Job that he must have sinned mightily to deserve punishment, but he maintains his innocence and asks his friends to pity rather than torment him as he recounts his woes in Job 19, including the abhorrence of kinsfolk and the wrath of God. Job is sure he will be vindicated in the end when he meets God.[28] Psalm 22 begins with God-forsakenness but ends with universal worship of God, who rules all nations. Its protagonist is scorned by evildoers who mock him, pierce his hands and feet, and cast lots for his clothes, but he still trusts God, as his fathers did, and cries out to God to deliver him.

20. Lord as Shepherd   Psalm 23   John 10

The Book of Psalms is the hymnbook from the temple in Jerusalem rebuilt after the Jews returned from exile. Composition of psalms was traditionally ascribed to David, and some go back to his time. Psalm 23 is a favorite. Jehovah is portrayed as a shepherd whose sheep lack nothing since he provides green pastures, waters of rest, refreshment of life and right paths on which he accompanies them.[29] Even when predators threaten death, the LORD protects the sheep with rod and staff, allays fear, and provides a verdant plateau. With head anointed with oil and an overflowing cup, the sheep is assured that goodness and kindness will be his lot all his days as he dwells in the LORD's household.[30] John 10 depicts Jesus as a good shepherd. Unlike the thief who sneaks into the sheepfold or the hireling who flees when the wolf comes, the good shepherd guides the sheep who recognize his voice, provides abundant life, and sacrifices for them. Jesus claims to be Son of God whose oneness with his Father is exhibited in doing God's work and protecting the sheep God gives him.

---

[27] The *Satan* is a kind of prosecuting attorney in the heavenly court.

[28] Job knows his *Go'el* lives, who will restore his rights, redeem, defend him in court.

[29] Hebrew *nephesh* rendered better as "life" than "soul." God's name is his presence.

[30] Hebrew *chesed* rendered "kindness." *Erech yamim*, "length of days" (not "forever").

21.   Forgiveness   Psalm 51   Luke 15

Though the wish for Jerusalem's walls to be rebuilt is post-exilic, the plea for mercy after sin in Psalm 51 suits King David's mood after Nathan exposed his scheming to get Bathsheba.   The psalmist confesses sin as an inborn condition and as a concrete transgression and asks that God would hide God's face from his sins and wash him whiter than snow. Offering a broken and contrite heart as sacrifice, he asks that God would create in him a clean heart and right spirit.[31] The parables of Jesus often tell us indirectly about God, sometimes being illustrated by divine outreach from Jesus himself. In Luke 15, God is portrayed as a shepherd who pursues a lost sheep, a woman who searches for a lost coin, a father who restores a prodigal son. Although the son confesses his sin and asks to be demoted to servant the father has compassion, runs to him, embraces and kisses him. There is no blaming sheep, coin, or son for being lost but superlative rejoicing for being found. Like the Pharisees who object to Jesus being with sinners, only the older brother keeps a score of wrongs.

22.   Time and Eternity   Psalm 90   Ecclesiastes 3

People live but a few decades, says Psalm 90, and then they are gone back to the dust whence they came. They flourish like grass in the morning and are withered by evening. God sweeps them away sighing. Ecclesiastes, also included in the Writings, takes a surprisingly cynical viewpoint. There is no progress and no superiority of man to beast. They are alike creatures of dust and breath; all is vanity.[32] Eternity is in man's mind but he cannot fathom it; it belongs to God. God is from everlasting to everlasting, our refuge in all generations. A thousand years in God's sight is but an evening gone. Because what God does endures forever changelessly, there is room for everything. There are times for birth and for death, for sowing and reaping, for lauging and weeping, for mourning and dancing, for silence and speaking, for love and hate, for war and peace. Since you cannot change the world or avoid death, you should live to the utmost within limitations.   For man to eat, drink, and enjoy work is God's gift. Establish, O God, the work of our hands, prays the psalmist.

---

31 Hebrew: *ruach* "spirit" (also wind), *kon* "upright" (firm, constant, steadfast)
32 Hebrew: *hebel*, "vanity," means to be like exhaled breath, transitory, empty.

23. Praise   Psalm 100   Psalm 150

Psalms 100 and 150 are exuberant hymns of praise. In couplets in which the second line repeats or extends the theme of the first line, these psalms exclaim where, why, how, and by whom God is praised. God is praised in the sanctuary as pilgrims bring a thank offering through temple gates and into its courts, coming into God's presence with singing and blessing God's name, who made a name for himself in the exodus and made his name to dwell in his house. God is also praised in earth and heaven. The whole earth is called to make a joyful noise to Jehovah, and God is praised in the vast firmament[33] of the overarching sky.   God deserves praise for God's goodness and steadfast love and everlasting faithfulness, for mighty deeds of deliverance and exceeding greatness. God is praised with human voice and dance accompanied by tambourine, by lute, harp, and other strings, by pipes, by trumpets, by cymbals resonant and loud. Since God is not only shepherd of God's congregation and lord of God's people but creator of all, Jehovah is praised by all that breathes.

24.   Wisdom and Help   Proverbs 3   James 2

The Book of Proverbs is a collection of wise sayings similar to those of non-Hebrew Near Eastern folk. Some proverbs extol wisdom itself. Wisdom was involved in the design of earth,[34] and likewise it takes discernment to map out the heavens.[35]   More precious than silver, gold, and jewels, wisdom brings long life, riches, honor, steadiness, confidence, fearlessness, pleasantness, happiness, peace, repose. The truly wise person is not wise in his own eyes but humbly and reverently trusts in the LORD and takes to discipline as a son to a father. Loyal, faithful, and not contentious, she is readily generous to God and neighbor. She does not merely pray that a person lacking clothes and food be warmed and filled, adds James 2, but gives what is needed if it is in her power. Showing no deference to the rich over the poor, who are special to God, she fulfills the royal law to love neighbor as self. Putting mercy before judgment, she exhibits her faith in works of obedience and rebellion as did Abraham in offering Isaac to God and Rahab the harlot in hiding Israel's spies.

---

33 Hebrew: *raqi*, a firm, solid overarching dome with embedded stars and rain valves.
34 Hebrew *chakmah* and its Greek equivalent *sophia* are both feminine.
35 Hebrew *t-bunah*, "distinguishing," harks back to God separating elements in creating.

| 25. | Vision | Ezekiel 37 | Jeremiah 31 |

The same prophets who foresee Judah's destruction also envision its reconstruction. Ezekiel sees Israel rising from the grave of exile in Babylon to new life in its own land in terms of dry bones being knit together with sinews, covered with flesh and skin, and inspired with breath and with the Spirit of God.[36] Like sticks bundled together, the former kingdoms of Israel and Judah will be united as a faithful people under a Davidic king attending God in the sanctuary through an everlasting covenant of peace. In this covenant, says Jeremiah, the law will be written not on tablets of stone but upon human hearts. The steadfast love of God for Israel will endure as long as the fixity and far as the vastness of the heavens and her sins will be forgotten. If anyone sins, his sins will end with himself, and children's teeth will not be set on edge because of sour grapes their fathers ate. In place of mourning for lost children, there will be joy and merriment and dancing and praise to God who has gathered his scattered flock. The city of Jerusalem will be rebuilt, and pilgrims will visit Zion.

| 26. | Restoration | Ezra 6 | Nehemiah 9 |

From a post-exilic priestly point of view, the chronicler retells the history of Judah up to the exile in two books of Chronicles and tells of rebuilding the temple and walls of Jerusalem in Ezra-Nehemiah (a single scroll in the Hebrew Bible). Cyrus king of Persia defeated Babylon in 538 B.C. and a year later authorized the rebuilding of the temple at royal expense and the return of the vessels taken from it. After many delays a modest temple was completed under King Darius in 515 B.C. and was dedicated to God with joy and a huge sacrifice. The people of Israel fasted and confessed their sins in sackcloth and ashes, and priests extolled God as maker of heaven, earth, and seas and recounted how God had been faithful to Israel through thick and thin. They related God's choosing Abraham and promising him occupied land, God's making a name for himself by defeating Pharaoh and rescuing the Hebrews, God's leading and feeding them in the wilderness and giving them law, God's forbearance as they turned from him, God's giving them over to their enemies, and God's bringing back a remnant.

---

36 The same Hebrew word *ruach* means both "breath" and "spirit."

27.   Promise   Isaiah 40   Isaiah 9

The book of Isaiah falls into two parts. Chapters 1-39 come from the pre-exilic Isaiah of Jerusalem while chapters 40-66 derive from a post-exilic source dubbed second Isaiah. Isaiah 9 speaks of God's judgment on his wayward people but also of hope for a time of light when it will no longer be the people who are burned as fuel for the fire but the warrior's boots and bloody civilian clothes. Isaiah 40 proclaims an everlasting God, creator of the ends of the earth who stretches out the heavens like a curtain. Before God, nations, princes and people are like grass or grasshoppers who wither and fade when Jehovah blows upon them. God rules with strength and tenderness, comforting his people after their long exile, feeding his flock like a shepherd, and renewing the energy of those who wait upon the Lord. Now that her warfare is ended and her iniquity pardoned, Israel is called to prepare the way of the Lord, for the glory of the Lord will be revealed to all flesh. A child will be born who will sit on David's throne and usher in an era of everlasting justice and peace.

28.   God's Triumph   Daniel 7   Revelation 19

Apocalyptic literature envisions God overcoming a present oppressor and ending human history by establishing his own permanent rule.[37] A great deal of such literature was produced during the Greek and Roman occupation of Palestine. Some books, such as II Esdras, are in the Apocrypha; only Daniel and Revelation made it into the canon.[38] Written during the Maccabean struggle in the second century B.C., the book of Daniel envisions the successive Babylonian, Medean, Persian and Greek empires as four great beast emerging from the sea with ten horns representing ten previous Greek kings followed by a liitle horn, the current ruler Antiochus Epiphanes. God is portrayed as an ancient one who transfers dominion from the beast to a human. Revelation, written by John of Patmos during Nero's persecution of Christians, envisions the Word of God, who is king of kings, in blood-dipped robe leading heavenly armies against the beast who is thrown into a lake of fire. Multitudes sing "Hallelujah" because the Lord God Almighty reigns as they prepare for the marriage supper of the Lamb.

---

[37] The Greek name for Revelation is *Apo-kalypsis*, stripping "away" what is "hidden."

[38] The *Apo-krypha* ("hidden away') is a collection of books included in the Septuagint and Vulgate but not in the Hebrew Bible as canonized by a council of rabbis in 90 A.D. Hebrews and Revelation were included in the New Testament canon after much dispute.

29. Hope and Love   I John 3   I Corinthians 13

Just before Revelation at the end of the New Testament come the Catholic Epistles, which are directed not to particular congregations as with Paul but to the whole church under the names of disciples.[39] John portrays Christians as God's children, born of God, abiding in God by the Spirit, keeping commandments to believe in Jesus and to love one another, incapable of sin, which is lawlessness and the devil's work. Following the sinless Jesus who laid down his life, we do not hoard the world's goods but pass from death to life by loving. In the middle of his cautions to Corinth about speaking in tongues, Paul inserts a love poem. Without love, there is no point in speaking in foreign and ecstatic tongues or miraculous faith or self-sacrifice. Love is patient, kind, humble, easy-going, magnanimous, and hopeful. Love outlasts prophecy, tongues, and knowledge, superceding them like maturity succeeding childhood. We will know God completely[40] when we get beyond reflections and see God face to face and become like God. Faith, hope, and love all last long, but love is the greatest.

30. Incarnation   Luke 1   John 1

The same author compiles a narrative about Jesus in the Gospel of Luke and a history of the early church in the book of Acts. Luke 1 anticipates the births of Jesus and his cousin John the Baptizer. John's father Zechariah blesses God for visiting and redeeming his people by giving him a child who will prepare the way of the Lord. Jesus' mother Mary magnifies[41] the God who has blessed her and helped Israel by promising her a son who will be a Davidic king destined to uproot the proud, mighty, and rich and exalt the lowly. The Gospel of John seeks more to illuminate Jesus' significance than to tell his life story. In John 1, Jesus is recognized by John Baptist and by his own disciples as Lamb of God who carries the world's sins and as Messiah, King of Israel, Son of God, Son of man.[42] Instead of a birth story, the prologue to John gives a theological interpretation. The Word of God, which shaped creation and enlightens every person, became flesh and was tabernacled among us in Jesus, dispensing grace and truth to believers by empowering them to be born of God.

---

[39] Greek *katholikos*: universal.

[40] Greek *teleios*: complete, perfect, finished, reaching the goal (*telos*), all-inclusive.

[41] Greek *megalunei*, Latin *magnificat*: to recognize greatness.

[42] Greek *christos*: anointed as king. "Son of God" is more than royal appointment here.

31.   Birth of Jesus   Luke 2   Matthew 2

Whereas Luke-Acts is addressed to a Greek, Theophilos, and features Jesus as universal savior and Paul as missionary to the Gentiles, Matthew is directed to a Jewish Christian audience and stresses the fulfillment of Old Testament scriptures as in the places of Jesus' birth and boyhood, the slaughter of innocents, and return from Egypt. Legends surrounding the birth of Jesus occur only in these gospels and share no details in common. Luke has Mary and Joseph going to Bethlehem, David's city, for a census, Mary giving birth to Jesus in a stable because no inn had room, angels extolling divine glory and human peace, and shepherds responding to the angelic announcement of the birth of their Savior-Messiah-Lord[43] by visiting the babe. Matthew has wizards from the East follow a star till it illuminates the place where Jesus is born and has them worship him by offering gifts of gold, perfume, and embalming spice.[44] After Jesus' bris (circumcision) and presentation at the Temple, Simeon takes him in his arms and thanks God for seeing salvation as light to the Gentiles and glory to Israel.

32.   Mission   Mark 1   Luke 4

The Gospel of Mark is the earliest gospel and the basis for much of the material in Matthew and Luke. Mark begins with Jesus' public ministry. Jesus began as an associate of John, who baptized him, but developed his own sense of mission after John was arrested. Mark sees Jesus' baptism as being anointed by the Holy Spirit to be messiah, the son of God.[45] That Spirit drives Jesus to the wilderness where he clarifies his calling as not being economic, religious, or political. Instead Jesus sees the Spirit anointing him to preach good news to the poor, release to captives, sight for the blind, and liberty to the oppressed in a favorable time when God's rule is breaking in (perhaps a year of Jubilee).[46] Jesus calls people to start over and believe this good news. Instead the people of his hometown synagogue threw him out. People were astonished at the authority and freshness with which Jesus taught, called followers, liberated the possessed, and healed the sick. Jesus did not stay put but stayed true to his purpose by announcing and demonstrating the kingdom of God as he visited cities in Galilee.

---

[43] Greek *kyrios* (Hebrew *adonai*): lord, reference to God. Earliest creed: Jesus is lord.

[44] Myrrh: an embalming spice, an odd gift for a baby unless in legend prefiguring death.

[45] Greek *christos*, Hebrew *messiah*: anointed. "Thou art my son:" coronation formula.

[46] In the year of Jubilee, ancestral lands will be returned restoring equality: Lev. 25.

33.   Abandon   Mark 2   Luke 7

Jesus confounds expectations. Many folks rejected John the baptizer as overzealous. They did not respond to John's dirge any more than to Jesus' dance. But at least John was a recognizably religious figure with his ascetic diet and frequent fasts and call to judgment. Jesus was not. The Pharisees also fasted and kept sabbath lawfully and avoided contamination. Not Jesus. He lacks religious scruples. His disciples help themselves to grain on the sabbath, which Jesus sees as a celebration of human freedom. They do not fast while the bridegroom is with them, for new wine requires fresh skins. Jesus heals the lover[47] of a Roman centurion and calls a tax collector to follow him. He comes eating and drinking, befriends tax collectors and sinners while being at odds with the good who do not need him. He is charged with blasphemy and immorality when he forgives sins of a paralytic that he heals and of a woman who shows hospitality, being forgiven much because she loved much. When asked if he is the expected one,[48] he notes freeing blind, lame, lepers, deaf, dead, poor.

34.   Commissioning   Mark 3   Luke 10

Gospels have distinctive emphases. Mark has Jesus keep a messianic secret silencing those who would prematurely reveal his identity. Luke stresses Jesus' outreach to foreigners. He alone tells the story of the Good Samaritan, portraying not the priest or Temple official, who avoid evil, but the despised Samaritan, who rescues and cares for the man robbed and beaten, as the one who really loves neighbor. Both Mark and Luke have Jesus commission disciples. Mark has Jesus single out twelve men as successors to the twelve tribes of Israel. Luke has seventy sent in pairs, including women, who share in Jesus' teaching and in the bonds of discipleship, which supplants family. Traveling without provisions, the apostles are to rely on their hosts, eating and drinking without distinction with any who receive them and proclaiming to all the approach of God's kingdom. In mission, the disciples rejoiced that diabolic and demonic powers were dethroned and defanged while Jesus rang judgment on towns more inhospitable than Sodom, towns which did not notice or respond to the Holy Spirit at work.

---

[47] Greek *entimos*. "The officer liked this servant very much (Luke 7:2b, CEV)."

[48] Greek *erchomenos*: the one who is coming, the messiah.

35. Kingdom of God   Mark 4   Matthew 5

God's word on Jesus' lips is like a sower sowing seed on rocky ground, shallow ground, among thorns, on good soil. Not everyone responds. Before him evil recoils like a storm subsiding at his word. As herald and demonstrator of God's kingdom, Jesus revises the law with authority. God's ruling nips evil in the bud, dispelling the anger that festers into murder and swearing turning into false witness and lust leading to adultery. God calls us to be like God, all-inclusive,[49] sending sun and rain on all, loving enemies, overcoming evil with good. Belonging to God's kingdom we turn persecution into blessing, refusing to be humiliated by inviting a fist on the left check after the right cheek is slapped,[50] exposing injustice by standing naked in court when stripped of our coat, walking an extra mile to protest being impressed as soldier's porter. As God's kingdom breaks in through Jesus, he brings happiness to the destitute, mourners, the gentle, merciful, pure in heart, peacemakers. His folk are salt of the earth, light of the world, a mustard seed starting small, getting big.

36. Rebirth   Mark 5   John 3

Unlike Mark, the Gospel of John portrays Jesus with a fixed identity evident from the first to those to whom it is revealed. Mark sees Jesus as a wonder-worker, expelling a legion of demons that occupy a man like the Roman legions who oppress the people, feeling loss of power as the hemorrhaging woman touching him was healed, calling a child to rise and eat who had been given up for dead. Allied with the faith of those he aids, Jesus finds himself involved in marvelous happenings but is reticent to claim credit or special powers himself. Not so in John, where the church's faith most overlays Jesus' life. There Jesus presents himself as God's only Son, sent by the Father to redeem the world, a heavenly man who descends to earth from above and enables people to sense the kingdom of God when they are born from above because the boundless Spirit blows through their lives.[51] While those who reject the light condemn themselves, life eternal abounds in those who receive the Spirit from the Son, whom God gave to the world and lifted up (upon a cross) out of God's great love.

---

49 Greek *teleos*: attaining the goal, complete, all-encompassing, reaching out to all.
50 The left hand being excluded as unclean, the available right hand could not slap again.
51 Greek: *anothen* means both from above and anew; *pneuma* means both wind and spirit.

37. Bread of Heaven   Mark 6   John 6

In contrast to the portrait of Jesus in the Synoptic Gospels,[52] John's Jesus is verbose and repetitive, always talking about himself, mired in endless disputes, not with particular parties, but with "the Jews," which is odd since Jesus himself was Jewish.   Obviously, later disputes between Christians and Jews have insinuated themselves into the story along with interpretations of later Christian practices.   There is surely some reference to Communion in Jesus saying that he is the bread of life come down from heaven that nourishes life eternal; John has Jesus say that his flesh is food and his blood drink and that he will enter those who take him in.   Less obviously, the feeding of thousands also refers to the miracle of Communion.   Throngs seek Jesus' company and help and perhaps would make him king, and even when Jesus tries to get away for solitude and prayer, they follow.   Although Jesus rejects supernatural stunts as a base temptation, his overcoming evil is pictured as walking on the sea.   Herod Antipater's execution of John the Baptist leaves Jesus seen as John's successor.

38. Freedom and Purity   Mark 7   Galatians 5:1-6:5

Neither Jesus nor Paul cares about keeping the external Jewish law, such as washing hands or eating kosher food or circumcision.   What is impure is not what goes into a person's body but what comes out of the heart, such as: anger and murder; lust and adultery; jealousy and covetousness; envy and theft; drunkenness and deceit; pride, selfishness, and idolatry.   The heart that cannot see beyond its own flesh[53] is embroiled in strife while the heart ruled by God's Spirit fulfills the whole law by loving neighbor as self.   From the Spirit come love, joy, peace, patience, kindness, goodness, faithfulness, gentleness, self-control.   True freedom is not beneath the law but above it, setting external law aside in order to be ruled by grace, crucifying self-limited passions so that Spirit may have free rein. Free folk serve each other in love, bearing the other's burdens, and so fulfill the rule of Christ in them.   Freedom knows no limits, for anyone may be reached and healed, even the Syrophoenician woman, and anything is possible, as even the deaf hear and the dumb speak.

---

52 Greek: *syn-optikos* = see together. Matthew, Mark, and Luke have much in common.

53 Greek: *sarx*. Sins of the flesh are not especially carnal but lacking a higher purpose.

39.   Suffering   Mark 8:1-9:1   Hebrews 2

The Letter to the Hebrews is not a letter but a sermon directed not to Jews but to Christians in a time of persecution, perhaps in Rome. Revered in the eastern wing of the church, it was not accepted as scripture in the West until the fourth century. Writing in polished Greek, its anonymous author proves points by citing the Septuagint[54] frequently. Here Jesus is portrayed as a high priest who sacrifices himself to expiate the people's sins. As man, suffering and tempted, Jesus is able to help fellow humans by tasting death for every one and in overcoming death delivering those long bound by fear of death. Perfected through suffering, Jesus pioneers the way to salvation. Those who follow him must also deny themselves and take up their crosses, says Mark's Gospel, for only those who lose life save it. Reflecting a perspective informed by later events, Jesus is seen as messiah,[55] who will come again soon in glory and power, but first is subjected, to Peter's consternation, to rejection, murder, and rising, crowned with glory and honor because of the suffering of death.

40.   Transfiguration   Mark 9   II Corinthians 5

To outward appearances,[56] Jesus was a landless peasant artisan turned itinerant healer and teacher, but to select disciples he is revealed as God's son, worth hearing, fulfillment of the law and the prophets, heir to Moses and Elijah, who appeared in John the Baptist heralding the last days but was executed. To disciples' puzzlement, the son of man is also slated to be killed and then to rise again.[57] Jesus models being first by being last and servant of all, reaching out to children, including an epileptic boy he heals, encouraging all other healers and the faith and prayer which enhances healing. Excising whatever causes sin[58] and living no longer for themselves, followers of Jesus, such as Paul, let the love of Christ control them. Judged by the heart and not by position, they are in Christ a new creation, reconciled to God in a right relationship through Jesus offering himself as a sacrifice for sin. Conducting a ministry of reconciliation as ambassadors for Christ in the power of the Spirit, they hope to be reclothed in a heavenly body as life swallows death.

---

54 The Septuagint: Greek translation of an expanded Hebrew Bible.
55 Greek: *christos*, "anointed one," chosen by God to rule in his behalf.
56 Greek: kata sarkan, "according to the flesh," from a human view.
57 "Son of God" commissioned by God; "son of man" ushers in final age.
58 Mark graphically mentions cutting off body parts to avoid Gehenna, a burning dump.

41.   Servanthood   Mark 10   John 13

Martyred by the time Mark wrote his gospel, James and John shared the cup of suffering and mortifying baptism of Jesus, who headed to Jerusalem where he would be mocked, scourged, killed, and raised,[59] but special places in God's kingdom were not theirs for the asking. After a rich man refused to sell his possessions to follow Jesus, Jesus remarked that it is as impossible for a rich man to enter God's kingdom as for a camel to go through the eye of a sewing needle, yet God can do what God wills. God's kingdom belongs to children. The rulers of the Gentiles lord it over them, but the greatest in Jesus' camp is the slave, who, like Jesus, came not be served but to serve. Jesus washed his disciples feet and commanded them to do so also. Jesus is about to go where his disciples cannot follow, for Judas will betray him and Peter will deny him, but Jesus leaves behind his example and, seeing love as the hallmark of discipleship, commands his followers to love each other as he loved them. Love between spouses rules out breaking their God-given unity through divorce.

42.   Authority   Mark 11   Romans 13

The kingdom of God has no need for forceful government or organized religion. Kings and priests are superfluous; they belong to the world that is dying. When Jesus comes to Jerusalem at Passover time, he engages in demonstrations, bits of guerrilla theatre. He enters the capital city, meek and lowly, riding on a donkey, and the multitudes hail him as the promised messiah strewing the road with garments and palm fronds. He enters the Temple, which colludes with the Romans in robbing the people, and disrupts its business. Jesus extols the power of faith and the need to forgive. When the Pharisees question the authority of Jesus, he will no more tell them than they will declare whether the work of John the Baptist was human or divine. In face of charges that Christians are disloyal, Paul writes the church in the capital city encouraging outward obedience to government as ordained by God--though soon to be superceded as light dispels darkness and provision for ordinary life becomes secondary when putting on the Lord Jesus. Love is all one owes anyone, for love fulfills all laws.

---

[59] Greek *ana-stasis*, literally "standing up" or "standing again," hence resurrection.

43.   Cornerstone   Mark 12   I Peter 2

The Gospel of Mark focuses more on Jesus' deeds than on his words. Mark 12 collects several sayings and places them in the context of Jesus' conflict with religious leaders. Jesus disparages scribes who make a show of religion and rich people making large offerings and discounts Davidic descent as a basis for messiahship. He praises the widow whose offered pittance is all she has and says that women will be men's equals after the resurrection. He affirms loving God and loving neighbor as self as the greatest commandments and lauds the scribe who raises love above sacrifice. He exposes those trying to trap him into endorsing or opposing taxes by showing that loyalty to Caesar has eclipsed their loyalty to God since they tote idolatrous coins engraved with Caesar's image. Jesus portrays God as taking a vineyard away from those tenants who killed God's servants and son and giving it to others, for whom the rejected stone has become the cornerstone of a new spiritual temple attended by a holy priesthood. I Peter counsels Christ-like submission to government and masters.

44.   Final Judgment   Mark 13   Matthew 25

Inserted into the thirteenth chapter of the Gospel of Mark is "the little apocalypse."[60] In imagery redolent of the Book of Daniel, the destruction of the temple, which occurred in 70 A.D, is seen as the first of many signs and tribulations portending the end of the age. Persevering under persecution and fleeing a desecrating sacrilege,[61] Christians are to expect false messiahs, which troubled times evoke and let the Spirit speak through them when on trial. No one but God knows when the end will soon come, but like maidens awaiting the bridegroom's arrival, they should keep their lamps filled with oil. When the final reckoning comes, those who made good use of the talents God has given them will be rewarded while the one who hid and returned his single coin will be cast out. Salvation comes not to those who, like the pharisees, seek it by separating themselves from the unclean in order to maintain ritual and moral purity, but to those who unknowingly serve Christ by feeding the hungry, clothing the naked, welcoming strangers, and visiting prisoners and the sick.

---

60 Verses 6-8, 14-20, 24-27, especially, are unlikely to have come from Jesus' lips.

61 Caligula had his statue put in the temple in 40 AD; Christians fled Jerusalem, 70 AD.

45.   Last Supper   Mark 14   I Corinthians 11

Jesus' Last Supper becomes the Lord's Supper and vice versa. Jesus' last meal with his disciples is archetype for Christians celebrating a sacramental meal at all times throughout the world. Jesus is host. In bread broken and wine poured, Jesus shares himself sacrificed, body and blood, and affirms a new covenant of redemption sealed by his self-giving. In the upper room, Jesus prefigures his death and anticipates drinking wine again with disciples in God's kingdom; in the Lord's Supper, Jesus' death is enacted and his return expected. While Paul argues with the Corinthians in favor of women covering their heads when speaking in church,[62] he bases his teaching on the Lord's Supper on tradition and demands more respect. Before supper, Jesus defended a woman anointing him for burial with costly nard. After supper, he prayed in Gethsemene to avoid death but accepted God's will. After Judas had betrayed him with a kiss, Jesus was arrested, examined, and condemned by the high priest for claim to be messiah.[63] Peter watched Jesus' trial but three times denied knowing him.

46.   Crucifixion   Mark 15   Isaiah 53

In Marks' Gospel, Jesus' disciples are not present at his crucifixion. With eyewitnesses sparse, the portrayal of Jesus' final hours is heavily colored by Old Testament scriptures. The suffering servant song in Isaiah 53, which applied originally to Israel in exile, is seen as fulfilled in Jesus. As a sheep being shorn is dumb, so Jesus did not respond when charged by the Roman governor and executed--as the indictment sign on the cross noted--for being King of the Jews. He was despised and rejected as soldiers decked him with a crown of thorns and mocked him. He was numbered with transgressors, a crucified thief reviling him on each side.[64] Jesus refused the drug offered to dull pain but was given vinegar to keep him alive in case Elijah rescued him. God-forsaken, Jesus cried out a psalm to God.[65] The curtain of the temple was split exposing the holy of holies. A centurion exclaimed that Jesus was a son of God. Surely God's servant, says Isaiah 53, has borne our griefs. God laid on him the sins of all; with his stripes we are healed and accounted righteous.

---

[62] Paul has a patriarchal hierarchy: God, Christ, man, woman;whores had shaved heads.

[63] This trial portrayed does not fit the rules governing the Sanhedrin.

[64] Luke has one thief befriend Jesus; in Mark the crucifixion is bleak.

[65] Jesus did not call Elijah, as his mockers pretended, but began to recite Psalm 22.

47. Resurrection   Mark 16   I Corinthians 15

The stories of Jesus' post-death disappearance and appearances are unique to each source and inconsistent with each other. Paul is keen on resurrection for Jesus and others as central but knows nothing of an empty tomb, which appears later in Mark as secret kept from fear. Women who had watched Jesus' crucifixion from afar and saw him entombed came the next morning to embalm him and were surprised to find the big rock sealing the tomb rolled away and no body there. They were told that Jesus was risen and would see them in Galilee.[66] Paul emphasizes the tradition that Jesus died for sins, was buried, and was raised, as scripture attests, the third day and then appeared to Peter, twelve, 500, James, and Paul.[67] Humans who bore the image of Adam,[68] the man of dust and death, will bear the image of Christ, the heavenly man. When the risen Christ returns, all powers will be subjected to him, including death. As the last trumpet sounds, the dead will be raised imperishable, clad in immortal spiritual bodies, like a seed buried in the earth coming to life in new glorious form.

48. Ascension   Luke 24   Acts 1

The Acts of the Apostles is a sequel to the Gospel of Luke as is clear from their first chapters with both books addressed to Theophilos.[69] Luke has the women who came to Jesus' tomb and other disciples who visited it later perplexed at Jesus' disappearance. Two of them walking on the road to Emmaus expressed dashed hopes that Jesus would redeem Israel and amazement at his absence from the tomb. They shared this with a stranger, who opened up the Hebrew Bible[70] concerning the necessary suffering and rising of the messiah. They recognized him as Jesus when he broke bread in a communion meal. Later Jesus stood among his disciples replete with flesh and bones and ate fish. After appearing during forty days, Jesus promised that the Holy Spirit would come upon his disciples, charged them to be his witnesses in Jerusalem, Judea, Samaria, and to the end of the earth, and then was lifted up into heaven whence he would return at a time unknown but to God. After Judas' death, his place among the inner circle of twelve disciples was filled by lot by Matthias.

---

66 Endings to Mark beyond verse 8 [snake-handling] are not in ancient manuscripts.
67 Scripture means the Hebrew Bible, the only scripture around at that time.
68 In Hebrew *Adam* is a generic term for man meaning earthling (*adamah* = "ground").
69 Theo-philos ("lover of God"), an unknown Greek; Luke wrote for a Gentile audience.
70 Referred to in terms of its parts: Moses (law), prophets, and psalms (writings).

49.   Christ's Spirit   Acts 2   Philippians 2

On the day of Pentecost, according to Acts 2, the Holy Spirit came upon the disciples like the sound of a mighty wind and with tongues as of fire enabling them to preach the gospel in many languages.[71] Paul exhorted the Philippians to have the same mind as Christ Jesus, who did not retain equality with God but emptied himself as a man by becoming a servant, humble and obedient unto death on a cross. For this reason, God exalted him so high that everyone will confess to God's glory that Jesus Christ is Lord.[72]   Likewise a spirited Peter preached to the men of Israel that Jesus had done mighty works, was delivered up according to God' s plan, was crucified and resurrected, was exalted by God to wield God's power as Lord and Christ,[73] and, as prophesied by Joel, has poured out the Spirit now seen and heard. Converts were told to start over and be baptized in Jesus' name and were promised the Holy Spirit. The disciples held goods in common and took care of needs. Working out their own salvation with fear and trembling, the Lord was at work adding daily to their numbers.

50.   Church Universal   Acts 7   Acts 10

Christianity was an offshoot of Judaism. In a sermon recorded in Acts 7, Stephen recounts the holy history of the Jews but sees it coming to a bad end in their murder of Jesus. God calls Abraham to a land of promise, leads Joseph and his brothers to Egypt where favor was replaced with slavery, spares the infant Moses from exposure, calls Moses to deliver his people and gives him the law on Mt. Sinai. But the people make a calf and worship it and replace the tent of witness with Solomon's Temple though God does not dwell therein. Receiving the law but not keeping it, they kill prophets sent to them. Envisioning Jesus at God's right hand and asking forgivenss for them, the crowd stones Stephen to death with the complicity of Saul, who would become Paul the apostle to the Gentiles. Peter was reluctant to associate with non-Jews, but having a vision of God commanding him to eat non-kosher foods, he met the Roman centurion Cornelius. Peter proclaimed Jesus as a healer anointed and raised by God. When the Holy Spirit was poured out on the Gentiles, Peter baptized them.

---

[71] Greek *glossa*, tongue:here speaking in foreign languages not ecstatic nonsense speech.

[72] This *kenosis* (self-emptying) poem was included by Paul's from an earlier source.

[73] *Kyrios* ("lord") is a substitute for God's name; *Christos* is messiah, God's anointed.

51. Body and Vine   I Corinthians 12   John 15

Paul sees the church as the body of Christ with members belonging to him and to each other, caring, suffering, and rejoicing together, shielding the less presentable members, prizing their diversity for the unique contribution each can make. Jew or Greek, slave or free, all have been baptized in one Spirit which enables them to confess Jesus as Lord in unison and to express severally a variety of gifts:[74] teaching, healing, miracles, prophecy, tongues, help, administration. Love is a still more excellent way; without it gifts are worthless. John sees Jesus and his disciples as a vine and branches with limbs bearing fruit because they abide in Jesus. Calling them not servants but friends, Jesus lays down his life for them and commands them to love each other as he has loved them. Spurning the system of world domination,[75] they can expect hatred and persecution like Jesus. Yet the fullness of Jesus' joy will be theirs as well. The teachings and love of God, which Jesus shared with them, will be amplified by the Counselor, the Spirit of truth, which God will send to witness to Jesus.

52. Consummation   Revelations 21   Romans 8

John of Patmos envisions a new Jerusalem coming down from heaven gilded and bejeweled like a bride adorned for her husband. God will dwell with us rendering a temple superfluous, and God's light will replace sun and moon. Gone are night, pain, death, and sea. God, the first and last,[76]will give water to the thirsty and sonship to victors. Paul pictures the whole creation groaning like a woman in childbirth waiting with eager longing for liberation from bondage to decay just as we who have been infected with God's Spirit groan inwardly to be freed of fear and to identify with a suffering Christ as sons of God. There is no condemnation for those who keep God's law by relying on the Spirit rather than their own devices.[77] The God who raised Jesus from the dead gives life to mortal bodies through God's indwelling Spirit.   In everything God works for the good of those whom he has chosen to be like Jesus. Despite distress, we are more than victors, for nothing at all--not death or life, institutions or rules, present or future--can separate us from the love of God in Christ Jesus our lord.

---

[74] "Jesus is Lord" is the earliest creed; glossalalia (tongues) need interpretation.

[75] Greek *kosmos*: "world." Christians are in the world but disavow its violent values.

[76] Greek *Alpha* and *Omega*, the first and last letters of the Greek alphabet.

[77] Greek *kata sarkan*: "according to the flesh," not referring to body but to godlessness.

Printed in the United States
123734LV00001B/75-76/P

9 781434 362100